TWO DUTCH COUPLES DURING WORLD WAR II

DECENCY AND LUCK

Virginia
thank you for your
interest and all
the work you do for
O h i will
Julia Oversloot Burg
April 2017

JULIA OVERSLOOT

•

Published by SO&SO Co LLC
Reno, Nevada
www.soandsoco.com

•

Production Assistant: Vicki L. Tam
Cover by Aspen Kuhlman

•

Library of Congress information available upon request
ISBN 978-1-938332-21-0

---

1   A little idea to write about the family during World War II became bigger and bigger culminating in a book called "So We Don't Forget" which was in two volumes ("Volume 1 – Life in the Netherlands" and "Volume II – Life in America"). There were 50 copies made through the Lifescapes program of the Osher Lifelong Learning Institute under Extended Studies at University of Nevada in Reno. All were distributed to family. It had as much information about the family as I could find and a timeline of historical and family events. This brief version was suggested by Robert Krell, "Now that you have done all the background work how about writing a book." So this is for the general public and concentrates on two family's lives during World War II – the Oversloots and the Krells.

This book is dedicated to all the "Righteous Gentiles" who were silent about their own stories of Decency and Luck.

Contents

I Kept Silent

When the Nazis came for the Communists,
I kept silent.
After all, I was no Communist.
When they came for the Social Democrats,
I kept silent.
After all, I was no Social Democrat.
When they came for the trade unionists,
I kept silent.
After all, I was no trade unionist.
When they came for the Jews,
I kept silent.
After all, I was not a Jew.
When they came after me—there was nobody left
who could protest.[2]

Reverend Martin Niemoeller 1937.
{U.S. Holocaust Memorial Museum
MM-courtesy of Bildarchiv Preussischer
Kulturbesitz, Berlin, Germany and
Martin Niemoeller widow.}

This very famous poem written by Pastor Martin Niemoeller, a German opponent of Nazism imprisoned in Germany from 1937 to 1945, and a concentration camp survivor.

---

2   Gilbert, Martin, *Never Again: A History of the Holocaust*, New York, NY, pg 178.

Acknowledgments

Special thanks to Robert Krell for his information and encouragement. Without his help, this book would not have been written. A big thank you as well to the Holocaust Memorial Museums in both Washington D.C. and Israel for providing documentation for this book. In addition, my siblings, Jeannette Huffman, Johanna Jurgenson, Jack Oversloot, and Jenny Floyd were very helpful with information and photographs. A special thanks to the many relatives in Holland, England, and France. My thanks to Sue White for her initial editing and guidance provided along the way.

I am indebted to the Osher Lifelong Learning Institute at the University of Nevada, Reno for offering Lifescapes classes and inspiring us to write and publish our memories. Thanks also to Margo Daniels and Joyce Starling, for shepherding my first book publish August 2011 through this process.

Preface

"For the dead and the living, we must bear witness."[3]
– Elie Wiesel

*T*his story is about an ordinary couple who did extraordinary things that could have killed them and their children in the blink of an eye. A Dutch couple who lived in Holland (The Netherlands) during the Holocaust protecting a Jewish couple who in turn protected their infant son. They did not hide the Jewish couple but incorporated them into the family. It is the story of the normal lives of a Gentile Dutch family in the worst of times. It is a story of "Decency and Luck."

The Author

I, Julia Oversloot, am the youngest daughter of Jacob (Jaap) and Jeltje (Jel) Oversloot. Born in The Hague in 1945 after the war. I am a banker, not a psychiatrist, historian or writer. However, I have a heightened sense of observation developed from receiving non-verbal cues from my family and others. It has serviced me well to determine when to listen, when to talk, and when to act.

Growing up, I was afraid to learn too much about the time of WWII in Holland. The silence of my parents and siblings reinforced the idea that I did not want to know. I just knew the atrocities were more than I could handle and still live a normal life. I avoided movies, books, and television program about the war. I knew movies did not really show the real horror of the time and how the people really suffered. It was not until my children were grown and out of the house that I started very slowly

Julia Oversloot Berg

---

3   U.S. Holocaust Memorial Museum letter of March 2011, speaking about Elie Wiesel, for "what he called the *living memorial.* Elie wrote a single sentence, so profound that we have inscribed it in stone on our walls."

to tolerate the stories. Schindler's List was a movie I know I needed to watch and I could only handle it in 15-minute increments. Then in 2008, I visited Anne Frank's home in Amsterdam with my daughter. I could barely talk and I tried to hide my tears. The dam had broken. From that moment on, I wanted to know how my family survived and why so many others had not.

Goal

To tell the story about family that had a clear sense of what is right and wrong and what represents decent behavior. I write in order to contribute to my father's goal, "*So We Don't Forget*"[4] and for those who were unable to write their stories.

Obtaining Facts

There are four versions of the story: my father, Eliasz (Leo), Estera (Emmy or Em), and Robert (Robbie or Rob). Each has a different slant and adds details to the chronological events. Their individual words are in *italics*. Words in brackets "[ ]" are to clarify those quoted sentences. I have inserted passages from books to compliment or expand on aspects of a story.

I sought help from newspaper articles, letters, the interviews with my siblings, my father's written speech to various Jewish assemblies, plus my father's video and audio recordings obtained from the Holocaust Museum in Washington D.C. and from Israel. In addition, the written testimonies provided by Robert, Leo and Emmy were indispensable.

I was able to interview my three sisters and brother to add some of what they remembered. They had not talked about the occupation until their interview with me.

---

4   From Woods, Arthur article in the Altadenan/Pasadena Chronicle dated April 7, 1983, "*So Don't Forget.*" See APPENDIX.

List of Who's Who

Eliasz (Leo) Krell — Jewish husband, father and furrier who has lived in the Netherlands since the age of one.

Estera (Emmy) Stelzer-Krell — Jewish wife, mother and immigrated from Poland in 1933 to the safe and neutral country of The Netherlands.

Robert (Rob) Krell — Jewish hidden son from the age of 2 to 5.

Jacob (Jaap) Oversloot — Christian husband, father and furrier who is self-educated and became the main bread winner for a family of seven at age 12.

Jeltje (Jel) Steiger-Oversloot — Christian wife, mother of four, who started making a living at age 11 as a seamstress.

Jantje (Jeannette) Oversloot — Oldest daughter who was between the ages of 6 to 11 during the war. She has the best knowledge of what happened during the war. She is a person who finds it hard to say "no" to anyone.

Johanna Oversloot — Second oldest daughter who was between the ages of 4 to 9 during the war. She has a negative view of life but a good memory.

Jacob (Jack) Oversloot — Middle child and only boy, was between the ages of 2 to 7 during the war. Silence to him means survival.

Jeljte (Jenny) Oversloot — Daughter who was a newborn at the beginning of the war. Despite her severe hearing handicap she has always been a positive thinker and happy.

Julia Oversloot — Youngest daughter who was born just a few weeks after the war ended as predicted.

Albert (Vader) Munnik — Christian foster parent to Robert Krell.

Violette (Moeder/Let) Munnik — Christian foster parent to Robert Krell.

Nora Munnik-Lorier — Christian foster sister to Robert Krell.

Johanna, Jeltje, Jeannette, Julia, Jack and Jenny in 1950

Testimonies and conversations of interviews dates are listed below and will be in italics and not footnoted.

Testimonies/Letters/Interviews

Eliasz (Leo) Krell — "Testimony of Leo Krell" letter. Complete testimony located in the Appendices section of this book.

Estera (Emmy) Stelzer-Krell — "Letter to Granddaughters" by Emmy Krell, 1985. Complete letter located in the Appendices section of this book.

Robert (Rob) Krell — Interviews by Julia Oversloot on 13 July 2010 and in 2011.

Jacob (Jaap) Oversloot — From Jacob Oversloot's combined stories. See REFERENCES for source details.

Jantje (Jeannette) Oversloot — Letter, dated 26 March 2009 from Sacramento, California, age 75 and interview by Julia Oversloot on 27 April 2009 in Sacramento, California, age 75.

Johanna Oversloot — Interview by Julia Oversloot on 29 September 2009 in Highland Park, California, age 73.

Jacob (Jack) Oversloot — Interview by Julia Oversloot on 2 August 2009 in Reno, Nevada, age 71.

Jeltje (Jenny) Oversloot — Interview by Julia Oversloot on 9 September 2009 in Wetumpka, Alabama, Age 69.

Family Trees

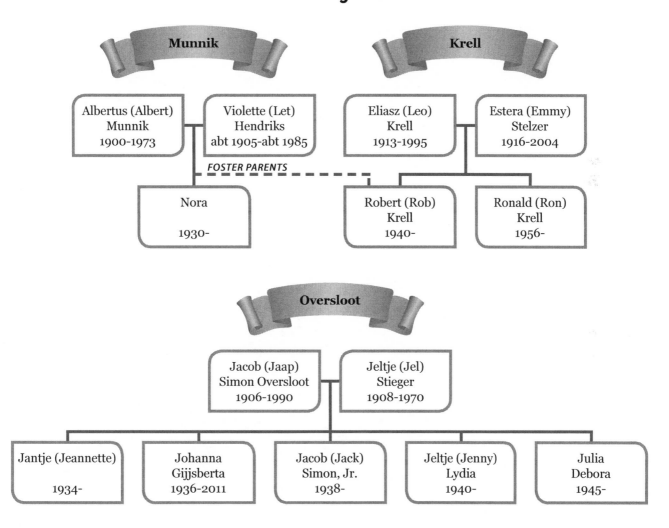

Munnik

| Albertus (Albert) Munnik 1900-1973 | Violette (Let) Hendriks abt 1905-abt 1985 |

Krell

| Eliasz (Leo) Krell 1913-1995 | Estera (Emmy) Stelzer 1916-2004 |

FOSTER PARENTS

Nora
1930-

Robert (Rob) Krell 1940-

Ronald (Ron) Krell 1956-

Oversloot

Jacob (Jaap) Simon Oversloot 1906-1990

Jeltje (Jel) Stieger 1908-1970

Jantje (Jeannette) 1934-

Johanna Gijjsberta 1936-2011

Jacob (Jack) Simon, Jr. 1938-

Jeltje (Jenny) Lydia 1940-

Julia Debora 1945-

Prologue

"On 1st of September 1939, without any warning, the Germans started a war with Poland. Germany had been preparing for years to start the thousand-year Reich —their plan to rule the world. Hating the Polish people as they did, Germany invaded Poland and with their superior weapons, they were able to occupy the defenseless country within two weeks.... Then the Germans turned against France, Belgium and Holland." [5]

— Estera (Emmy) Krell

The Great War 1914-1918[6]

The Great War was between Germany, Austria-Hungary, and Ottoman Empire facing the Allied powers of Great Britain, France, Russia, Italy and Japan. The U.S. joined the Allied Powers in 1917, which changed the course of the war. The Treaty of Versailles was signed in June 1919.

Of the many provisions in the treaty, the most important and controversial required Germany to accept sole responsibility for causing the war and to disarm, make substantial territorial concessions, and pay reparation. This would prove to be a factor leading to later conflicts, notably and directly to the start of the Second World War.[7]

The honorable thing for Germany to do would have been to honor the treaty its representatives signed. The major world powers could have stopped Germany from preparing for war by enforcing the terms of the Treaty of Versailles as each violation occurred. Instead, no enforcement took place. Some of the violations were: [8]

---

5 See APPENDIX for the complete "Letter to Granddaughters" by Emmy Krell, 1985.
6 www.history.com/topics/world-war-i
7 www.Wikipedia.org/wiki/'TreatyofVersailles'.
8 www.Wikipedia.org/wiki/'TreatyofVersailles'.

- 30 June 1930 France withdraws its last troops from Germany's Rhineland, five years earlier than the date set by the Treaty of Versailles.
- 13 Jan 1935 Germany regains the Saarland from France.
- 1 March 1935 Germany introduced compulsory military conscription and the rebuilding of the armed forces.
- 7 March 1936 Hitler reoccupies the demilitarized zone of Rhineland.
- 12 March 1938 Hitler annexes Austria in the Anschluss.
- 15 March 1939 Hitler occupies the rest of Czechoslovakia, Prague, Bohemia and Moravia.
- 1 Sept 1939 Hitler invades Poland thus initiating WWII in Europe. Atrocities against Jews began in every occupied town.

    "Approximately 3,300,000 Jews lived in Poland before the outbreak of World War II. It is estimated that over 3,000,000 of them perished in the Holocaust." [9]

But why was there no enforcement or consequences to these violations?

After the Great War, each major power came back home and found they needed to solve their own domestic problems. Simply stated below are some quick facts during this time:

- 1918 The United States Senate did not pass the Treaty of Versailles, which contained the Covenant of the League of Nations. U.S. President Woodrow Wilson urged passage.
- 1919 Race Riots erupted in 26 cities
- 1919 September Woodrow Wilson fell ill and for 17 months was unable to act as President
- 1920 Ottoman Empire dissolves
- 1922 Italy becomes a Fascist government

---

9   Oliner, Samuel and Pearl, The Altruistic Personality, The Free Press, NY, 1988, pg 25.

- 1926 Father Coughlin made his first radio broadcast beginning his 20-year career of racist and right wing politics.
- 1929 N.Y. Stock Market Crash that started the Great Depression
- 1929-1933 President Herbert Hoover was blamed for the Great Depression
- 1930 Unemployment soars. March 1932 unemployment rose to 13 million people
- 1932 Russian (Ukrainian) Famine
- 1933-1945 Franklin D Roosevelt (FDR) became President and bought hope to the people
- 1934-1936 the Dust Bowl affected over 300 million acres in America
- 1936 Britain General Strike brings activity to a standstill
- 1936 War between China and Japan begins and continues to WWII
- 1939 WWII starts and FDR proclaims U.S. neutrality
- 1939 The SS St Louis with 900 Jewish passengers were turned away from Cuba and not allowed in a U S port
- 1941 Charles Lindberg steadfastly campaigned for non intervention in Europe
- 1941 Lend-Lease program is approved by congress and helped the war effort with ships and equipment—later with food
- 1941 Dec 7 The Japanese attacked Pearl Harbor

Once upon a time ...

"Before the war, we were all very happy living in a kind of fairytale, beautiful country, with a Queen who was called Wilhelmina and her daughter, Princess Juliana. Holland was a country of hard working people, involved with their families, loving their children, having respect for all kinds of religion and education. The government was supportive towards all kinds of churches, synagogues and schools. People had free choice to go to all of them or to any one of them."
— Estera (Emmy) Krell

*A*fter The Great War, there was fear in Europe that Germany would rise again. German economics were very poor and according to the Treaty of Versailles they were responsible to pay back a huge sum the German Government did not have. The German citizens were suffering from unemployment, lack of goods, and jobs. Their money was almost useless compared to other nearby countries. They needed someone to blame for all the bad things that happened to them, so they decided they would force the Jews to shoulder the blame. The Jews were smart people who stayed and held Germany together. They were the doctors, governmental leaders and shopkeepers. Non-Jews resented that the Jews had work when they did not. This kind of prejudice had been going on between *haves* and *have-nots* since the beginning of time.

This prejudice in Germany grew and grew until the famous "burning of books" in May 1930 and *Kristallnacht* in 1938. During this time, Jews were encouraged to leave the countries of Germany and Poland to live elsewhere to be safe and in a better environment.

Manya, Frieda, Leo and his Mother c. 1920 {K},

Yakov Avraham Stelzer and Kreindle Klausner before 1932 {K}.

Eliasz (Leo) Krell

Eliasz ("Leo") Krell's family left Poland when he was a one year old in 1914. They left so his father could avoid the draft into the Austro-Hungarian army. As part of the anti-Semitism of the day, Polish Jews were drafted into the military for 20 years in order to break up Jewish families. Leo's parents, Moses and wife came to Holland and lived in The Hague with their three children to keep the family together and experience religious freedom. Sometime before World War II ("WWII") something happened that is not clear. Moses was never given proper papers to live in Holland; as a result, he made a new life owning a bakery in Antwerp, Belgium.

Emmy and Leo Krell – Wedding Day in December 19, 1937. {U.S. Holocaust Memorial Museum, courtesy of Robert Krell.} Photo on cover.

Estera (Emmy) Stelzer-Krell

Estera ("Emmy") and her cousin left Poland in 1933 with a six months visitor's visa to come to The Netherlands ("Holland") to live with an aunt. Emmy could see what was coming—death and destruction in Poland. The Netherlands was known for religious freedom and had remained neutral during The Great War. Emmy begged her parents, Yakov Stelzer and Kreindle Klausner, to come with her brothers and one baby sister but to no avail. Emmy kept on renewing her visa to stay in Holland and soon it was impossible to go back to Poland.

Emmy and Leo met at a Jewish youth club and were married in 1937 in The Hague where they continued to live.

Life in The Netherlands before 1940

"Rotterdam is a city and municipality in the Dutch province of South Holland, situated in the west of The Netherlands. The municipality is the second largest in the country with Amsterdam the largest. The greater Rotterdam area, best known as … 'the Rhine's mouth' referring to Rotterdam's location at the end of the Rhine-delta and its economic position as Europe's main port, contains around 1.3 million people … . It forms the southern part of the Randstad, the sixth-largest metropolitan area in Europe, with a population of 6.7 million … . Rotterdam is on the banks of the river Nieuw Maas (New Meuse), one of the channels in the delta formed by the Rhine and Meuse rivers."[10]

This may be the last picture of my Dad's family before Pieter died. Believed to be taken in 1913 – father, Pieter (32), his wife Jantje (38), Johan (6), Jans (15), Nel (2), Jacob (7) and Pieter (8) – Jantje may have been pregnant with Hill who was born 6/11/13 and Hendrik was born later 12/15/15. {Photo provided by Sonja van Ee.}

The Oversloot family has lived in the Rotterdam area and nearby area for over 400 years. Many were laborers and sea captains. Most were Protestants.

The name *Rotterdam* derives from a dam on the Rotte River.

Jacob Simon (Jaap) Oversloot

Jacob (Jaap) Oversloot was born 31 May 1906 in Rotterdam. His grandfather, Pieter Cornelis Oversloot was a captain and his father, Pieter Cornelis Oversloot (Jr.), was a laborer on his dad's barge. Pieter, the son, later became a longshoreman.

When the British blockaded the Rotterdam harbor during The Great War, Jaap's father found work in the Merchant Marines. He transported

---

10 www.Wikipedia.org/wiki/'Rotterdam'.

sick and dying soldiers from the front to the hospitals along the rivers.[11] However, there were no precautions taken during that time to avoid catching the illnesses of those soldiers. No sterile gloves, gowns, or antiseptic were used on the boats. Pieter Cornelis became ill with meningitis and died three days later on April 23, 1916. He was 34 years old. His son Jaap, was 10 years old. His mother, Jantje, had seven children by then and was "stranded" in Rotterdam.

Jaap recalls that they were as "poor as church mice" in a very true sense. His brother Pieter was a year older, Johan was a year younger and his two sisters at home were 5 and 3 years old and Henk was only 5 months old. Jans, the oldest sister, was working as a domestic in exchange for room and board. They got food from the government and Uncle Coos and Aunt Dirkje paid the rent. They lived on other people's charity. Even though they were poor and only wore hand-me-down clothes, they were surviving.

Jaap started to find small jobs and eventually quit school at age 12 to get more work. In Jaap's spare time, he read books to learn. He could retain what he read because he had a bit of a photographic memory. This skill helped him his whole life. He was self-educated from this young age.

This is Jaap's words and story about his young life:

"When I was 15 years old [1921], *I worked as an errand boy for an uncle of mine. Later, no one thought it was a job with a future. So I went to my other Uncle* [Coos] *who was a furrier. I spent 4 years with him. I was still living at home during this time. I made a little money, not much, but it all helped a little bit.*

"I didn't see any progress or future in being a furrier. It would have been a long way off before I could make it my trade and make real money. I tried something else. I started a business with a little cart selling ice cream in Rotterdam.

---

11 In WWI, more than 70 million military personnel were mobilized with more than 9 million combatants killed, largely due to the great technological advances in firepower without corresponding advances in mobility. It was the second deadliest conflict in history. {www.wikipedia.org/wiki/World War I.}

That did not go well. My eldest sister [Jans] *got married and lived in Amsterdam, so I move there to sell ice cream. It did not do any better there. So then, I started working for a factory that refined sugar from beets. It was a seasonal job. All the beets came out of the ground in the winter to go to the sugar factory. I worked for a couple of months there.*

"*Then one way or another I was back in Rotterdam. From there, I found a job as an intermediate furrier. I went from one place in Rotterdam to another because the work was very seasonal. Actually, I was good for nothing. I was a helper – a pair of hands. One year I worked in Rotterdam, then in Leiden, then The Hague, and eventually went to Haarlem where I met my wife. We went to Amsterdam* [together] *where we started working for a big department store.*

"*After a while, when I had more knowledge and experience, the department store transferred me to The Hague store. I got married; we had some children.*"

Jaap was proud he was never without work, even through the Depression. Here is a summary of Jaap's work history from ages 14 to 36, along with the addresses and title letters of recommendation that he brought to America:

Age 14, 1920 to April 1924, *from C Oversloot (uncle)*, (Bontwerker) Kruiskade 32, Rotterdam

Age 18, 10-19-24 to 12-06-24, *from H Pypeman*, The Holland Fur Trust Stationsweg 318, Rotterdam

Age 18, 12-1-24 to 4-10-26, from *(director)*, N.V. Handelmy Debenhams, Lebenhams Holland (Debenham Co), Holland, 47-53 Lange Voorhout, The Hague

Age 19, Ltr dated 01-07-1927, *from M Misse*, Het Bonthuis (Geise & S Rotmann), Nieuw Rijn 25, Leiden

Age 19, 6-13-27 to 5-12-28, *from E Cohen*, Het Bonthuis, Heligeweg 47, Amsterdam

Age 21, Around 1929 to 1942, Maison de Bonneterie, Den Haag

Age 36, 1942 to Sept 1950, *from E Krell*, Bontwerkerij Krell (the partnership), Spui 149, s-Gravenhage

Johanna Gijsberta Middelkoop Steiger–Jeltje's Mother in costume.

Lieuwe Steiger–Jeltje's Father c. 1948.

Jeltje ("Jel") Steiger

Jeltje was born 23 February 1908. She was the youngest of three children. She adored her big brother Jan Johannes Steiger ("Jan") and they were close their whole lives. Jel disliked her sister Johanna Marie Louise ("Joopie") Steiger because she made life very hard at home for Jel. She lost touch with Joopie shortly after she was married and moved to Germany.

Jel's mother Johanna Gijsberta Middlekoop was born in Amsterdam. Lieuwe, Jel's father, was born in Dongjum, Franekeradeel in Friesland. They were married 28 July 1897 in Amsterdam. His occupation at that time was a "smith." It was believed he may have been a dental apprentice, but the family only remembers him selling flowers from a cart.

Jel's father, Lieuwe must have been physically or verbally abusive and/or drank a lot. After being married, Jel made a strict rule to only see him once a year. He would always give her fresh strawberries, her favorite at those visits. Lieuwe must have had some good qualities because Jan named a son after his father.

Jeltje Starting to Earn a Living[12]

It was the custom at age 14 that you could go to work, go to a trade school or to a university prep school if you had high enough marks. The Steigers did not have money to send Jel to a trade school or a university. So, she therefore went to work at Kahn & Loeb in Amsterdam, starting just before her 11th birthday [1919]. She saved up and used some of the money she made to pay for tuition at the Mode-Academie, a seamstress trade school. There she learned about different fabrics, sewing techniques, how to make a pattern, cut and sew men's suits and shirts, women's dresses, lingerie, plus children's clothes.

For the final exam, she was given three dolls, cutout of clothes from magazines, and told to make those clothes for the dolls by hand, using crepe paper. Her tasks were to

---

12 Oral discussion with Jeltje Oversloot over the years.

sew a woman's dress, a man's shirt and a young girl's sailor dress. She passed with flying colors and a diploma was issued in Haarlem on June 22, 1925. The diploma qualified her for a job as a master seamstress.

In September 1925, she used her degree to go to work for A.Weill sewing fur coats in Haarlem, while still doing piecework for Kahn and Loeb until 1929. At age 21, she left home and moved into an apartment in Haarlem with a girlfriend.

At the apartment, Jel met a good-looking young man, named Jacob (Jaap) Oversloot who had recently started a new job in Haarlem. They had said "Hello" many times in the halls as they passed. One day Jaap asked if Jel would like to go to dinner and they walked and talked for hours. Jaap enjoyed Jel because she was so much fun and was always laughing at something. He knew she was a hard worker like himself and when she had a little extra money, she splurged on pastries or cloth to make clothes. They eventually were in each other's company every weekend hiking, visiting friends, going on walks and talking.

Jaap moved back to live with his mother in Rotterdam after he was transferred to the Bonneterie in Den Haag around 1930.

In September 1929, Jel took a job with E Kahn at the Maison de Paris in La Haye, to be near Den Haag and Jaap. In 1930 she worked for Bont-en Pelterijenhandel, in Den Haag.

Before they were married, they traveled to the German Alps. Eventually both Jaap and Jel worked at the Bonneterie.

Here is a summary of Jel's work history from ages 11 to 22, along with her letters of recommendation:

Age 11, 02-02-1919 to 08-31-29, *from Kahn,* Kahn & Loeb (Pelterijenfabrick), Keizersgracht 389, Amsterdam

Age 17, The Seamstress Diploma was issued June 22, 1925

Age 17, 09-01-25 to 02-02-29, *from Wilhelm Loon,* A. Weill (Bontwerker), Barteljorisstraat 26028, Haarlem, *This must have been where Daddy met Mom.*

Jeltje at about 18 years old c.1926.

Age 21, 09-23-29 to 04-05-30, *from E Kahn,* E.Kahn/Maison de Paris, 29 Hoostraat, La Haye

Age 22, 04-07-30 to 08-30-30, *from Jean Geets,* Bont-en Pelterijenhandel, Heerenstraat 21-23-23A, Den Haag

Age 22, 1930 to 1934, Maison De Bonneterie, Den Haag

Married Life Starting 1931[13]

Jel was in seventh heaven making her three-tiered silk wedding gown. She married at age 23, so she did not keep the pledge she made with her girlfriend to not get married until she was 25 years old. They were married 29 July 1931 at the town hall in Rotterdam, as was the custom. After the wedding, they lived with Jacob's mother Jantje in Rotterdam for a short time. For fun, they tried to make all the recipes in her old cookbook. By the time they moved, they both knew how to cook pretty well.

They moved to *Den Haag* and lived at 90 *Scheldestraat* and then at 220 *Allard Piersonlaan*. Both places were a three flat walk up. At one of these apartments, they became fast friends with a policeman and his wife, Truuse, who lived upstairs.

Jeltje soon became pregnant and was looking forward to her first child. It was to be a joyous event. However, December 9, 1932 a premature boy was born. It was what they called a "blue baby." In other words, it never took a breath, so the baby looked blue from lack of oxygen. Jel was very depressed and Jaap took extra care to bury the child by himself. The baby was never forgotten. Jel kept a lock of the baby's hair that she had sewn between two pieces of clear plastic and had it in her jewelry box her whole life. It was in her hand when she was buried in 1970.

Life continued and there were other joyous events to come. Jantje [Jeannette] was born August 3, 1934, Johanna Gijsberta was born February 5, 1936, and Jacob

Jaap and Jel's wedding photo, Rotterdam, 29 July 1931. Photo on cover.

---

13 Research from letters and family oral history.

Simon Jr. [Jack] was born January 22, 1938. Sometime during this time, Jel stopped working at the "de Bonneterie" as a seamstress.

In 1937, when Jel was cooking at the stove, the three-year old Jeannette needed her shoe tied. Jel leaned back too far and the back of her dress caught on fire. She screamed, and Truuse came down quickly and saw the problem. Truuse had Jel roll on the carpet to put out the fire. To remedy the burn, they wrung out tea-drenched cloth of very strong cooled tea on her back. The tea remedy would add tannic acid to reduce the amount of blistering. However, her back and part of her arm were scarred for life.

Jaap and Jel purchased a house at 20 Miquelstraat in Den Haag. Miquelstraat is a funny little street that zigzags. At one end, it opens to a main street and a place where shops like the green grocery, bakery, and cigar store were located. In the middle was a small square where children normally met to play. The street was lined with wall-to-wall houses, one of which was ours. Jaap made a drawing of the house before 1950 and it looks the same today.

Our House[14]

The house was built in 1929 and had a small front and back yard 18 x 16 feet. Across the street from our house were three garages for use by the whole neighborhood.

"Looking out the front window and seeing the Germans take the cars from the garages across the street," was one of Jeannette first memories about the war. We were privileged to have a car in one of those garages after the war.

Miquelstraat 20, The Hague 2008

As you enter the house, the front door hall was on the right and the living room on the left, behind is the dining room with a kitchen in the back. The stairs were straight ahead of the front door, which curved around to the left.

---

14 From an Internet search March 2011, I found our house was for sale at 199,750 Euros or about $275,000 U.S. at the exchange rate of 1.38. The description of the house had the size of the back yard in meters and at 39.27 inches per meter; I figured the size in feet. That meant the house was most likely 18 feet wide but very deep. Real Estate taxes are calculated on the frontage of the home.

The second floor had one large master bedroom (16' x 9') in the front of the house and two small bedrooms in the back. The attic was one large space. Under the stairs on the first floor was the only toilet. There was no shower or bath in the house. The siblings each remember getting buckets of hot water from the merchant down the street, Mondays for the wash, Wednesdays to clean the house, and Fridays for bathing. They put the bathtub in the kitchen for bathing and took turns by who was cleanest first.

Jenny remembers, *"Mom and Dad had the biggest bedroom upstairs and it had a separate heater. They may have partitioned the room off so I had my own space. I remember Jeannette and Johanna had one bedroom and Jack the other. Then there was the attic for Emmy and Leo plus the workroom. We were not allowed up there. All the fur machines and fur stretching equipment was up in the attic."*

Jack remembers, *"A little single green water heater above the kitchen sink. We only had one toilet. I am surprised we had that many people living in the little house. That had to be a tremendous amount of pressure for my parents. There would be the four children, Mom and Dad, Leo and sometimes Emmy, which is a total of eight people, plus all the meals Mom had to cook including lunch for the workman."*

I remember a story before the war. Jel and Jaap took the family out on bicycles to look for another house many times. However, they always seemed to have bad luck. 'Murphy Law' went into effect. There were accidents on the way – Jeannette fell off her bike, they had flat tires, etc. Jaap finally gave up and said, "We need to stay where we are but I don't know why yet." Actually, the places where they looked for new living quarters would **not** have kept them alive during the war. They were either bombed or not suited for Jaap and Leo to do so well in business during the war. Jel later said, *"It was God's will."* The house was a sanctuary for the Oversloot and the Krell families during the war.

Environment Before the War

"The people, in or about 1938 just before the war, were recovering from the big Depression. Business was picking up, it was very good, and there was work for the people. They knew a war was going to come. The people from Poland [refugees] came to Holland by the hundreds from the German pogroms because things were getting bad for the Jewish people. That was quite an activity just before the war."

– Jacob (Jaap) Oversloot

The chart indicates the number of countries where the German Jewish refugees went between 1933 and 1938 to escape German persecution."[15]

"Honoring its tradition of providing sanctuary to the persecuted, Holland admitted approximately 25,000 Jewish refugees from Nazi Germany, Austria, and Poland between 1933 and 1940."[16]

The chart indicates 30,000 German refugees came to Holland; that means 5,000 came from other counties like Poland. Estera Stelzer (Emmy who married Leo Krell) and her cousin were two of the admitted refugees from Poland.

"Since the domestic unemployment rate was high then, resentment developed against this influx of aliens and led to Holland's decision in 1939 to intern indigent German [and Polish] Jewish refugees at a camp in Westerbork in the province of Drente rather than grant them permanent asylum."[17]

Emmy was employed and therefore was not among those who went to Westerbork.

Refugee havens	
Countries taking in German Jewish refugees from 1933 to the end of 1938	
United States	102,222
Argentina	63,500
Britain	52,000
Palestine	33,399
France	30,000
Holland	30,000
South Africa	26,100
Shanghai	20,000
Chile	14,000
Belgium	12,000
Portugal	10,000
Brazil	8,000
Switzerland	7,000
Bolivia	7,000
Yugoslavia	7,000
Canada	6,000
Italy	5,000
Australia	3,500
Sweden	3,200
Spain	3,000
Hungary	3,000
Uruguay	2,200
Norway	2,000
Denmark	2,000
Philippines	700
Venezuela	600
Japan	300
Total	**453,721**

List of estimates of what countries the German Jewish people went to, from 1933- 1938 {NA pg 39 - Courtesy of Bildarchiv Preussischer Kulturbesitz, Berlin.}

---

15 Gilbert, Martin, *Never Again: A History of the Holocaust*, New York, NY, pg 39.

16 Oliner, Samuel and Pearl, *The Altruistic Personality*, The Free Press, NY, 1988, pg 32.

17 *Ibid.*, pg 32.

Jews in Holland

"In 1930 approximately 113,000 persons representing 1.4 percent of the population were registered as belonging to the Jewish faith in Holland. After Hitler's rise to power in Germany, a number of German Jews settled in Holland, enlarging the existing community to about 144,000 persons. Most Jews lived in the big cities. Amsterdam had a neighborhood largely inhabited by Jewish people. In contrast to the situation in Germany and in most Western European countries, Jewish Dutchmen engaged mainly in manual labor and belonged to the low-income group. For example, they almost held a monopoly as grinders [cutters] in the Amsterdam diamond industry. Many Amsterdam Jews such as street vendors belonged to the lowest stratum of urban society."[18]

Stockpiling

Jaap recalls, *"The merchants were importing all the staple foods and goods into Holland in preparation for the war. They were sure they would be neutral like in The Great War. They figured they had enough [stockpiled] goods to last five years. These imported goods would last, they would not be lacking goods like they did in 1914 to 1918 when there was a blockade and all exporting or importing was stopped. Every businessman was buying stuff to be prepared that there would be enough stuff for people to live on."*

Dutch Government before the War

"In the years between the First and Second World Wars, Holland enjoyed stable government.... Dutch foreign policy was designed to maintain the neutrality that had served The Netherlands so well during the First World War. The Netherlands depended on the maintenance of good relations with neighboring powers, especially with Germany and England, since trade with the German hinterland and with the Dutch East Indies – the security of which required the support of Great Britain – was the mainstay of the Dutch economy.

---

18 Warmbrunn, Werner, *The Dutch under German Occupation 1940-1945*, Stanford Press, 1963, pgs 165-166.

The Netherlands also made an effort to establish closer collaboration with other small countries of northwestern Europe, particularly neighboring Belgium.[19]

"Official relations between The Netherlands and Germany had been good up to the Nazi seizure of power. Common interest in carrying trade on the Rhine made cooperative relations mandatory. When international tension began to increase after the German Occupation of the Rhineland in 1936, the German Foreign Office repeatedly assured The Netherlands government that the Reich would respect Dutch neutrality. An explicit declaration to this effect was delivered in the last days of August 1939, just before the outbreak of hostilities."[20]

Emmy recalls, *"One day, our Prime Minister, Dirk Jan DeGeer,[21] talked to the Dutch people on the radio. His speech went like this, 'People of Holland, we have nothing to worry about; we are going to stay neutral; we are not going to war with anyone; we have no weapons to fight a war with, and to my knowledge we own only three planes. But we took steps to have plenty of food for our people to last about six years and these supplies are stored mostly in coolers in the*

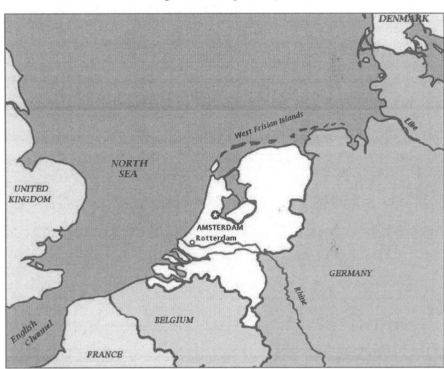

Map of The Netherlands and surrounding countries [www.yourchildlearns.com/ online-atlas/images/map of netherland.gif}

---

19 *Ibid.*, pg 3.
20 *Ibid.*, pgs 4-5.
21 Wikipedia - Emmy letter indicated Dr Willem Drees but he was not the Prime Minister until 1948, 1951-1952.

Port of Rotterdam.' Unfortunately, being an honest man, Mr. DeGeer had also revealed to the Germans where the food was stored. Mr. DeGeer finished his speech to the Dutch people with encouraging words to the effect that, 'We have very brave soldiers and the people to back them up to defend our beloved country."

"On August 28, 1939, the Dutch government ordered the mobilization of the armed forces in anticipation of the outbreak of war. Immediately after the invasion of Poland on September 1, 1939, the Dutch government issued a declaration announcing the intention of The Netherlands to stay out of the European conflict. The mobilization [at the borders] was maintained until the invasion [in May 1940].

"The state of war existing between Germany and the Allies imposed a heavy economic burden on The Netherlands, quite apart from the expense of mobilization. Transit trade with Germany practically ceased because of the British blockade. War conditions made it more difficult to secure raw materials for Dutch industry. Dutch ships were sunk by mines in the English Channel and elsewhere. As a result of the conditions, the total volume of industrial and commercial activity decreased. Unemployment rose despite the fact that approximately 300,000 men were mobilized."[22]

---

22 Warmbrunn, Werner, *The Dutch under German Occupation 1940-1945*, Stanford Press, 1963, pgs 4-5.

Invasion of Holland 1940

"Power corrupts, and absolute power corrupts absolutely." [23]
– Lord (John Emerich Edward Dalberg) Acton [1887]

"... [In 1939] Hitler was the head of the state, the government, the army, the judiciary and the Party, ... a state of absolute power ... " [24]
– Werner Warmbrunn, *The Dutch under German Occupation* [1963]

"The great masses of the people ...
will more easily fall victims to a big lie than to a small one." [25]
– Adolf Hitler, Mein Kampf [1922]

Adolf Hitler justified the violation of Dutch and Belgian neutrality on the basis of the need to protect the Ruhr Valley and to gain air bases or the coming attack on England ... . In a briefing of his top command, Hitler had stated brazenly that 'a breach of the neutrality of Holland and Belgium is meaningless. Nobody will question that when we have won ... .' The Queen issued a proclamation repudiating the German assertions and branding the invasion as a breach of international law and decency ... .

"Adolf Hitler had hoped to conquer the country in just one day, but his forces met unexpectedly fierce resistance. French forces in the south and British ships in the west came to help but turned around quickly, evacuating many civilians and several thousand German prisoners of war from the German elite airborne divisions." [26]

---

23 Bartlett, John, *Familiar Quotations, Fifteenth and 125 Anniversary Editions*; Little, Brown & Company, Boston, 1980, pg 615:15 from a letter to Bishop Mandell Creighton, April 5, 1887.
24 Warmbrunn, Werner, *The Dutch under German Occupation 1940-1945*, Stanford Press, 1963, pg 21.
25 Bartlett, John, *Familiar Quotations, Fifteenth and 125 Anniversary Editions*; Little, Brown & Company, Boston, 1980, pg 812:17. From Adolf Hitler, Mein Kampf, 1922, Vol. 1, Chp. 10.
26 Warmbrunn, Werner, *The Dutch under German Occupation 1940-1945*, Stanford Press, 1963, pgs 6-7.

How it Began - 10 May 1940

Emmy's story of the start of the war is, *"On 10 May 1940, Holland was attacked by the Germans. Aeroplanes, called 'Stukas', which looked like big black bats, bombed the cities. Parachuters from some of the planes dropped out of the skies disguised as Nuns, Priests, civilians, and hidden in their clothing were weapons to attack anyone who was in their way. The Dutch soldiers who were near the border between Germany and Holland tried to fight back. The Germans said, 'We are going to bomb Rotterdam and flatten it to the ground' and half of Rotterdam was burned and destroyed … . The Dutch soldiers were still trying to hold back the German invaders and so the Germans told the Dutch people to stop fighting or they would do that to other cities what they had done to Rotterdam.*

"It was like living through a nightmare; like a scene from a Spielberg movie—or even worse because it was really happening it was the real thing. That night, Queen Wilhelmina, Princess Juliana and Prince Bernard left Holland and went to England. The next morning on the radio, we listened to the announcer. His words were, 'Listen to the voices that are known to you. We are the Dutch people'—and [long] *silence. He was shot* [during his broadcast] *and the Germans took over the radio station and told us that we had no Government anymore and we were now all prisoners of war and everything would be alright if we just followed their regulations—but we did not know what their regulation would be or how harsh they would be. We were soon to learn."*

14 May 1940

"By Tuesday, May 14, the military situation had become manifestly hopeless. The Germans had cut off fortress Holland from Belgium and established themselves solidly near Rotterdam."[27] Because the surrender had not been signed fast enough the bombing of Rotterdam occurred.

"The center of the city, including one-eighth of the total area, was destroyed. Approximately 900 people were killed and 78,500 were made homeless. Rotterdam, along with Warsaw and Coventry, became wartime symbol of Nazi ruthlessness … . Thus, the Dutch had to give up the fight against an enemy who had planned a modern war for which The Netherlands was even less prepared than France or Great Britain. Dutch casualties in manpower had not been heavy, but the superior technology and greater resources of the invader had rendered further resistance useless. The people of Holland entered the five years of occupation after a five-day war which had been so brief that most citizens had not fully grasped what had happened."[28]

Rotterdam after the bombing 1940
{Provided by Willy de Swaaf Robson}.

---

27 *Ibid.*, pg 9.
28 *Ibid.*, pgs 9-10.

The Occupation

The effects of the Occupation on the daily lives of the Dutch people varied widely from one section of the population to another. Some continued in their normal daily routines until the final months of the war. In the early years particularly, day-to-day physical life, at least for the majority, remained as it was during prewar days, except for changes imposed by rationing and curfew regulation. Gradually more citizens were affected by the measures of the occupying powers until, by the last winter of the war, conditions created by the Occupation and by the conduct of the war dominated the lives of nearly all inhabitants of The Netherlands.[29]

"As a rule, farmers and others living in rural areas were less exposed to the new regime than were their urban compatriots. Many people in the country seldom met German soldiers or policemen. Conversely, those living in the largest cities had more personal contact with German officials than did the population of rural areas or of medium-sized and small towns. City-dwellers saw the N.S.B. [the Dutch Nazi party] in action more often, and they suffered more from rationing because they could not secure supplementary food directly from producers."[30]

May 1940 to Spring 1941

"The first phase of the Occupation lasted from May 1940 until the spring of 1941. Its first few months, at least, may be called the 'honeymoon' of the Occupation. Hitler allowed Dutch prisoners of war to return to civilian life. At this time German leaders were confident that they would conquer, without much additional military effort, those sections of the European continent that were not yet under their control. They established a German supervisory civilian administration for the occupied territory, headed

---

29 Warmbrunn, Werner, *The Dutch under German Occupation 1940-1945*, Stanford Press, 1963, pg 100.
30 *Ibid.*, pg 11.

by Dr. Arthur Seyss-Inquart.[31] This administration undertook the first tentative steps, which would lead to conflict with the population in subsequent years. Rationing of food and other goods was established gradually. Employment services began to recruit labor for work in Germany, but did not yet physically force Dutch workers to work in the Reich."[32]

Stockpiles Confiscated

Jaap stated, *"When the Germans, after three days, occupied Holland, [they] took all the staple products that had been imported from all over the world. The Dutch goods were shipped to Germany. So for the* [Dutch] *people themselves there was nothing left. There was no coffee, no tea—anything that had to come from outside was gone. The Germans paid for the goods, but with money that was not any good.*

"In June 1940, in order to stop the unlimited hoarding of goods in which many people engaged immediately after the surrender, German authorities ordered a registration of all supplies at the wholesale level. They also began moving them to the Reich, the raw materials and foodstuffs that the Dutch government had stockpiled as a precautionary measure. Seyss-Inquart intended to leave only enough supplies in The Netherlands to keep industry going for six months. By the end of that period he hoped to achieve the integration of Holland into the German war economy."[33]

---

31 Dr. Arthur Seyss-Inquart, a Dutchman, was head of the German supervisory civilian administration for the occupied territory of The Netherlands. He is most quoted in the book *The Dutch under German Occupation 1940-1945*, because the author's research is mainly from his notes.

32 Warmbrunn, Werner, *The Dutch under German Occupation 1940-1945*, Stanford Press, 1963, pg 11.

33 *Ibid.*, pg 70

"I can tell you a story about what happened. During the war, I was selling and doing business in furs. I had a neighbor who had a connection with another man. He put me and the other man together to talk about business and what was for sale. There were 50,000 moleskins somewhere in Amsterdam in a warehouse. I wanted to see the skins to set a price and check on the quality. I talked with the man who owned the skins to set a price. If you want to buy goods, you want to see what you are buying. After setting a price, I said, 'I will pick them up the next day and give you the money.' In the meantime, which I did not know, the Gestapo moved at night and confiscated all the 50,000 skins because they had belonged to the Jewish firm. They never paid a penny for it. So that was the way the Germans did business.

"[The] Germans confiscated all Jewish funds and property: 20% of their value was given to the [Jewish] Council, 80% was kept by the Germans as booty. At the same time all Jewish businesses were seized and more than 5,000 Jewish men were sent to forced labor camps throughout Holland."[34]

"In 1940, they [the Germans] *had more interest in getting all the goods out of Holland rather than the Jews out of Holland* [but they were building a list of Jews. The Germans administered Jewish institutions, schools, hospitals, temples, etc. The Germans had a devious reason for this.] *They only administered them long enough to get the address listing of all the Jews. As soon as that was done, all the Jewish institutions were closed."*

"Dutch officials unwittingly lent legitimacy to anti-Semitic laws by tacitly condoning them and supplying native bureaucrats and police to help implement them. Though clearly performed under duress, Dutch participation in the Nazi campaign against the Jews spared the Germans from deploying costly numbers of their own scarce personnel to enforce it."[35]

---

34 Gilbert, Martin, *Never Again: A History of the Holocaust*, New York, NY, pg 82.
35 Oliner, Samuel and Pearl, *The Altruistic Personality*, The Free Press, NY, 1988, pg 34.

Acts of violence in the streets

Jaap said, *"The Germans were very careful during the day. They didn't want the reputation that the Germans were bad. They would make raids in the middle of the night and after curfew.*

"The Nazis did not want to shock the Dutch sensibilities and provoke widespread resistance. Instead, they gradually disenfranchised, impoverished, and isolated the Jews in a period when German domination over Dutch Gentiles was still relatively tolerable, thereby dissociating the latter as much as possible from Jewish suffering."[36]

"They also made all kinds of laws. You [the Dutch Citizens] *have to turn in copper, brass, and your radios. Then the bicycles, then the blankets and things like that. They tried to get everything from the Dutch people."* That was between 1940 and 1942.

Emmy gave these details, *"We were not allowed to have a radio or a telephone; we had to give our bikes to the Germans; everything that was gold, silver or copper had to be given over to them—everything that was valuable was taken away from us. Then the Germans went after our lives. In the middle of the night they would pick up all the highly educated people first, they disappeared and nobody heard from them again. For the Jews they had even stricter regulation. They had to wear on their coats the Star of David, which made them visible, if they went into streets, which were restricted to them. They were arrested by the Germans and put into concentration camps."*

---

36   Warmbrunn, Werner, *The Dutch under German Occupation 1940-1945*, Stanford Press, 1963, pg 65.

Leo and Jaap become Friends

"In this time, the Jewish people were not allowed to do any business."
– Jacob (Jaap) Oversloot

Jaap tell this story, "After a little amount of time [in June 1940], the Dutch army was dissolved and soldiers went home. The officers were kept under arrest. One of those free soldiers [Leo Krell], I met in the store. He told me he was in the Army. He was ordnance [like military police] in the Army. The regular army had disbanded. He could go home and in the meantime, he was living in a temporary kind of camp. While he was there, he was starting to get a business together. He was making fur coats from scraps.

"I'm a furrier and Leo is a furrier. I worked in a big department store [Maison de Bonneterie in The Hague] and he worked in the open market where he sold furs from a little stall. His mother, a widow[37] and two sisters were also vendors.

"I was a supervisor of the seamstresses and some of them were Jewish and my direct chief (boss) was Jewish, and the owner was Jewish. All through the store were Jewish people. So, I knew quite a few Jewish people. What I figured out was that Leo was a Jewish man,"

"Awareness that people around them were Jewish may have reflected in part the greater tendency of rescuers to have Jewish friends."[38]

Leo Krell as a soldier in the Dutch army poses astride his motorcycle. {U.S. Holocaust Memorial Museum Archives #73215 courtesy of Robert Krell.}

---

37 According to Robert Krell, his grandmother was not a widow but she was separated from her husband who lived in Belgium because he did not have the proper papers to stay in Holland.
38 Oliner, Samuel and Pearl, *The Altruistic Personality,* The Free Press, NY, 1988, pg 115.

Jaap continues, *"Leo wanted to buy some parts of skins we did not work ourselves. We came to talk about the war and what he did with the parts of the skins he was buying. So I spoke to my department head … if it was all right with him if I gave this man first chance at those parts of the skins. And being a very nice man, my department head let me go ahead … . We sold him the leftovers. When he bought stuff, he would come to us.*

"I did business with him [Leo] and he did business with me. In this time, the Jewish people were not allowed to do any business. But I paid no attention to that rule. I didn't want to take orders from the Germans."

Becoming Friends

Jaap said, *"He [Leo] invited me to his home and we became more or less friends in a business way. When he came to buy stuff, we would get to talking and get to know one another. I sold some of his fur coats, which he made from the parts we sold him first. Our store being a very elegant department store, it was not easy for my friend to sell his coats. So I began to give him some of the paper models we prefer to use. That way we got our own material back, fur in our own designs, and he was making a nice living.*

"So, this Jewish furrier and I met each other more and more. I visited him at his home, with my wife and vice versa. So I [got to] know his wife [Emmy] and his little boy [Robbie] who was crawling over the floor. Note: In the 1987 video, Jaap was smiling and happy as he recalled Robert crawling on the floor. It was a very pleasant memory.

"We were friends by that time. I decided that I did not want to be told by somebody else what to do. If they tell me don't work for a Jew, don't sell things to a Jew, don't do this or that for a Jew—well I am an independent man and I will do as I please."

"Defying the Nazi rule of destruction in whatever
way possible is itself a moral victory."[39]

---

39 *Ibid.*, pg 112.

Separation between Jews and Gentiles

"Final solution is to kill all Jews"
– Hermann Göring

*J*aap stated, "When the Occupation happened, the whole Dutch government was taken over by the Germans and the Jewish people had to wear yellow stars of David and their identification papers were stamped '*Joden*' and [they could no longer use public] transportation on streetcars or buses. There were restricted shopping hours and Jews were not allowed more than 200 guilders in their possession. Jews in key positions were given special passes from the place where they work to go home again."

Spring 1941 to Spring 1943

"During the second phase of the Occupation, lasting from the spring of 1941 to the spring of 1943, the conflict between the German administration and the population of the occupied territory became more pronounced. This conflict resulted in part from the breakdown of the conciliation attempt, as evidenced by the February strike in Amsterdam and the severe punishment administered by the German Occupation authorities.

"The first overt demonstration of Dutch solidarity with the Jews came too early to actually help them … . In early 1941 [February], Jews in Amsterdam organized Action Groups to resist the marauders. In one such confrontation, Nazi party storm troopers called the Defense Troop [Weer-Afdeling or WA] were killed, prompting the Germans to retaliate by arresting 425 young Jewish men and banishing them to Mauthausen, where they were worked to death … . Moreover, this precedent and

> the German practice of taking and frequently executing Dutch hostages deterred most of the Dutch from actively opposing Nazi policies over the next two years."[40]

"The entry of the Soviet Union and the United States into the war against Germany during 1942 created the practical prerequisites for an allied victory. The growing likelihood of such a victory was bound to be encouraging the spread of Dutch resistance.

"The increased conflict was related to the radicalization of German policies after the invasion of the Soviet Union. Rationing measures became increasingly strict. Compulsory registration for all unemployed labor was established in 1942, and selected groups of specialists were more or less forced to work in Germany. In the spring of 1942, the Wehrmacht reinterred the professional officers of the former Dutch armed forces. The German police took hostages to be held responsible in the event of future sabotage."[41]

History of the Final Solution

"The earliest known use of the term 'Final Solution of the Jewish Question' was in an 1899 memo to the Russian Czar Nicolas II written by Theodor Herzl, author of the 1896 book, *The Jewish State*. Theodor Herzl is known as the father of Zionism. Nicolas II is regarded as an anti-Semite."[42]

Hermann Göring took charge of resolving the German 'Jewish Question' December 14, 1938." His "Final Solution" was to kill all Jews:

---

40 *Ibid.*, pg 36.

41 Warmbrunn, Werner, *The Dutch under German Occupation 1940-1945*, Stanford Press, 1963, pg 12.

42 www.wikipedia.org/wiki/Final_Solution

Final Solution Stage I began June 1941

"Stage I: The mobile killing units, or *Einsatzgruppen*, began their work June 1941. But the mass shootings were inefficient and psychologically burdensome to the killers. It became desirable to send the victims to the killers. Thus, killing centers were created at strategic railway junctions near the main Jewish population centers of German-occupied Poland.

Final Solution Stage II began December 1941

"Stage II: Mobile gas vans were used at Chelmno beginning in December 1941. The main drawback of the vans was their limited capacity. They could not handle large number of victims. They were also slow. The excruciating suffering of the victims, who died by asphyxiation, was of little concern to the SS, but the task of unloading the vans after each use was time-consuming and 'unpleasant'. Dying took so long that the anguished victims could not control their bowels and left a mess. From the summer of 1941 on, German authorities intensified their efforts to segregate and concentrate the Jewish population. In July 1942, they began to deport Jews to Poland.

Final Solution Stage III began March 1942

"Stage III: Stationary gas chambers were in operation beginning in March 1942. Within a few months, they were established at all the killing centers except Chelmno, which continued to operate with what was then obsolete technology. Two types of gas were used for killing: carbon monoxide and hydrocyanic acid, which was the agent of choice at Auschwitz-Birkenau. The gas chambers had a much larger capacity than the vans and could handle hundreds of victims at a time. They were more reliable … . At the height of the Hungarian deportations, as many as 10,000 Jews were gassed per day at Auschwitz."[43]

---

43 Berenbaum, Michael, *The World Must Know*, Johns Hopkins University Press, 1993, pgs 118-119.

These Final Solution Stages were suspected by the Dutch citizens and especially the Dutch Jews and some knew some of the facts. But it was not until the end of the war that evidence of murders became public knowledge. Even in the underground, the extent of the devastation was not known while it was occurring.

"In 1942, the concentration camps held 100,000 inmates. Their population grew geometrically; to 224,000 in 1943, and 524,000 in 1944. By January 1945, the concentration camps held 714,000 inmates, of whom more than 200,000 were women…. More than 3,000,000 people --mostly Jews-- were murdered in these camps, some by starvation, exhaustion, disease, shootings and beatings. But many more were killed by gassing."[44]

44 Warmbrunn, Werner, *The Dutch under German Occupation 1940-1945*, Stanford Press, 1963, pg 118.

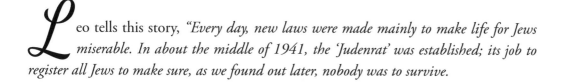

A Jew's Story of the Occupation

"The old Jewish story."

– Eliasz (Leo)Krell

*L*eo tells this story, *"Every day, new laws were made mainly to make life for Jews miserable. In about the middle of 1941, the 'Judenrat' was established; its job to register all Jews to make sure, as we found out later, nobody was to survive.*

"Beginning 1941, Civil servants were required to fill out forms indicating whether or not their grandparents were Jewish. Jewish businesses were identified for eventual transfer to German owners."[45] If your grandparent was a Jew, you would be classified as a Jew.

Leo continues, *"From here on we were harassed, the telephones taken out, bicycles and public transportation prohibited.* [We were required] *to wear a yellow star of David, shopping only after 5 pm when all was sold out, etc. – the old Jewish story."*

Between June 1941 and July 1942, "German administration ordered Jews to deposit their money in blocked accounts at a designated bank managed by German officials. Jews were allowed to withdraw from these accounts only small monthly allowances. They also were forced to register their real estate under German supervision and to dispose of it eventually [to German ownership]. The Germans authorized employers to discharge Jews and

---

45 *Ibid.*, pg 36.

prohibited Jews from exercising certain professions. Unemployed and later even employed Jews were sent to labor camps within The Netherlands." [46]

Leo continues, *"By June 1942, we knew already several people who were picked up by the enemy and did not return. At the same time, I had to appear first before the 'Judenrat' in Amsterdam, then for later visits to the Gestapo headquarters in the same place. They commanded me to return in a few days and deliver to them a list of my clients, list all furs in my possessions, bring my insurance papers, passport, documents and proof of all our possessions.*

"I had to fill out an application for Rob, Em and myself for what they called 'Vrijwillige Emigratie' [Voluntary Emigration]. Which I refused to do. Again, I got a few days respite. Rob was at that time not quite 2 years old."

Jaap's reaction to Leo's Plight

Jaap said, *"Jewish families received orders to go to [concentration camps]. Now it was time to worry about our Jewish friends, Emmy and Leo Krell. We knew that was the end and what that meant. We had heard enough by this time from all the people that had gone before.*

"All kinds of plans were made; maybe try to ride by train to unoccupied Switzerland or Spain. That was a long and hard way with a baby and the chance that those borders were open at all. People were picked up left and right. And there was no one to be trusted.

"Dutch Jews had already been placed in a natural trap." [47] The rivers, ports, and borders were blocked and the dense population had nowhere to go.

---

46 Warmbrunn, Werner, *The Dutch under German Occupation 1940-1945*, Stanford Press, 1963, pgs 63-68.

47 Oliner, Samuel and Pearl, *The Altruistic Personality*, The Free Press, NY, 1988, pg 33.

"My department head, with all his connections, tried to send his two teen-age daughters away. They were caught in Brussels, at their grandmother's, taken away and never heard from again."

Leo continues, *"We decided to leave it to the last moment. Maybe something would come up.*

"We had some good Gentile friends and by discussing with them the circumstances, we decided to fight, not to give in to any of the German Regulations."

"However, despite the reluctance to report to the Westerbork train, only a minority of the Jewish population attempted to avoid deportation by going underground. It has been estimated that approximately 20,000 Jews, or fewer than one out of six persons slated for deportation, went into hiding and that 8,000 of these survived, half of them children."[48]

The Krells were three among the 8,000 that went underground and survived.

Jaap and Jel's feelings about the Germans

Jaap states, *"When we heard our friends had to go to 'the East',[49] I talked with my wife. We decided, my wife and me, that that was a terrible thing. That Dutch people had to go to East for what? They were good people. They didn't do anything wrong. So we decided instead of letting them go, Leo was going to take off his Jewish star and that he should come to my place. In the meantime, I had a room made in the attic with a washbasin.*

"My feeling was that I hated the Germans very bad. Me and my wife decided that people had no right to do what they were doing. So we don't have to listen to them.

---

48 Warmbrunn, Werner, *The Dutch under German Occupation 1940-1945*, Stanford Press, 1963, pg 170.
49 In my dad's words, he said "Auschwitz" but Robert pointed out that it was unlikely that they knew the name "Auschwitz." That was post-war information. But the rumors were that "the East" was bad.

It was not our laws and rules. So we had no obligation to do what they told us. We could do everything just in the opposite. If they say you should not do this or that, we did it anyway."

Krells came to Live with the Oversloots—1942

Leo states, *"We lived in fear a few more months with a family who were our friends. We decided to use part of their attic and prepared it so that I could stay there without coming down too much. That family's name was Jacob S. Oversloot, his wife Jeltje, and there were four little children* [Jeannette, Johanna, Jack and Jenny]. *Em was supposed to stay where Robbie went, but things were to be different than planned. In this most strenuous time, we had another Gentile couple who visited our place practically every day to lend moral support and to help us if the need should arise. Her name was Mrs. Mulder and his name was Hol. 'Opa Hol' we called him. This was during the time no Gentiles were supposed to visit or collaborate with a Jew."*

August 18, 1942 and August 19, 1942

Leo goes into detail, *"On the evening of August 18, 1942, when curfew was 8 pm (no-one allowed outside after 8 PM), some men came to the front door to deliver three letters, stating that we had to be on 19th of August at 1:00 AM (really the beginning of the 20th) at the railway station for the first part of our last trip, to Camp Westerbork. The letter stated to take not too much and nothing heavy, but to take blankets, some clothing – I guess to make it look real. The actual idea was to get you out, close the door behind you, leave everything so that the Gestapo could pick it all up, and give it to the German people.*

"Our departure from home was planned for after 8:00 PM (remember the curfew). This was done by the Gestapo to undermine chances of avoiding the rules. Now the action started. We packed, mainly light made to look heavy. We put Rob in a buggy and left, with the neighbors watching. We left around 6:00 PM taking for granted that people would not know the precise time arrangement in our letters.

"We had a 10-minute walk to the house of Opa Hol and Mrs. Mulder. According to plan, Em and Robbie stayed there. I was supposed to go to J. Oversloot. All went well for a few days. When Mrs. Oversloot got sick and had to go to the hospital leaving her husband, four kids and me at home. We asked Em for help and she did help. She left Rob for a few days with the Mulders and joined the Oversloot household. Em looked after the four kids, the men, the cleaning, everything-but had no chance to see Rob. The German roundup of Jews, the curfew, and all the troubles together took a few weeks. Our contact with Rob was through Jaap Oversloot. He came home from the Mulder's telling us he is well, looks good and doesn't cry."

The Hidden Child — Robert Krell

Robert remembers nothing until he had to leave his parents. But how did this come about?

"My family's date of deportation was 19 August 1942 – from The Hague, presumably to Westerbork and then to Auschwitz. Rather than risk that mysterious eastbound venture into the unknown, my parents bravely opted to give me away. For three years, I lived in hiding with a Dutch family, angels unbeknownst even to themselves."

Robert (Robbie or Rob) Krell

In a letter written to her granddaughters, Emmy tells this story. "[Robert] *decided to be born, August 5th, 1940 in the middle of a big air raid, and on the same day, that Princess Irene was born.[50] When I arrived at the hospital, the nurses who, like most Dutch people, loved our Royal Family told me that if the baby was a girl I must call her Irene. [The baby] was a boy and I could hardly have called him Irene! So he was named Robert.*

"In every ward in the hospital there was at least ten hungry mothers as the other wards were full of wounded German Soldiers. We got very little to eat as the food supplies were given to the solders. We were afraid of the nights as that was when the city was attacked from the air. Yes, we were hungry and frightened but we had our babies and our husbands filled our rooms with flowers to let the Germans see that we were not losing hope. We were not much to the Germans but we meant a lot to each other. We were loyal to our country and helped each other every way we could. Sometimes sharing food, even though we had so little to share. We knew that we had to survive but our future did not seem very secure."

---

50 Research indicates that Princess Irene was born 5 August 1939, one year earlier.

Find a Place to Hide Robert

Jaap said, *"Mr. & Mrs. Krell when they came to our place they had a little son. Also, my family was at that time four children and two adults. Robert was the same age as my daughter.* [Jenny and Robert were 7 months apart in age both born in 1940.]

"They could not be sister and brother because they were so close in age. My little girl was a blond, real typical Dutch girl. His little boy, Robbie, was nice and dark [haired] *Jewish boy. We could not pass them as belonging to the same family. We could not have that boy at our place."*

In her letter, Emmy continues, *"On 19th August 1942, when Robbie was two years old, it was our turn to go to a camp with 6,000 other people including parents and children. But we met some nice people during the summer who were willing to help us but they could only take the parents as they already had four children of their own and so another family took Robbie. To be separated from your child is a very hard thing but we wanted badly to save his life and this was the only thing we could do. We prayed the separation from our son would only be for a short time because there was talk of a 'Blitz Krieg'—a short war. We never thought about losing the war even with the Germans occupying our cities and treating us very harshly. We had something higher to believe in than just Hitler—we had our religion and we were not killers— we believed in the commandments—'Thou Shalt Not Kill'—because killing is not the solution to anything.*

"Your Daddy [Rob] *lived six-weeks with a lady called J.Mulder who had also a little boy of 11 and an old gentleman who was called Opa Hol. He* [Robbie] *did not like it very much to be away from his parents."*

Leo continues, *"But now the big news came. Opa Hol and Mrs. Mulder were called in by the German decree, which wanted all older people out of the city. They were willing to take the child but we protested. We did not want to take our chances outside The Hague.*

Emmy and Robert Krell- A Dutch-Jewish mother plays with her young baby seated in a high chair c.1940-1941. {U.S. Holocaust Memorial Museum #73217, courtesy of Robert Krell.}

"We then got a message that Mulder and Hol had friends whom Hol used to work with. They would take Rob, no questions asked, knowing we were Jewish. We met those wonderful people and they were the three Munniks, Let and Albert Munnik and their daughter Nora who was 12 years old. The Munniks told us not to worry. If they ate, Rob too would eat and that while bringing up their daughter, they would temporarily bring up a son, until times got better. Then they would give him back."

According to Robert, Albert [Albertus] and Let [Violette] Munnik just happened to visit the Hols the day they were looking for another place for him. What Luck! He felt it was a blessing to have such wonderful foster parents who loved him so much. They would have been willing to make him part of the family if Emmy and Leo had not survived.

Emmy wrote, *"[Nora and Robbie] shared a room and we were very lucky that the little girl was not jealous of the little boy and she accepted him and loved him more than if he had been her little brother. She taught him to read at the age of four, played with him, and taught him to do all kinds of things. It was a difficult task to keep the little boy a secret from the neighbors for he wanted to go out to play. If it were found out that the little boy should have not been living with this family it would have meant a lot of trouble for them and they were very brave people as their lives were at stake and the Germans would have dealt harshly with them.*

"Some neighbors knew the boy from before but we were lucky that they were on our side and they did not belong to the Nazi party and so the boy was safe and the people who had taken him in were safe. Finally, he came to believe that the people he stayed with were his parents and his real parents were known to him as his Aunt and Uncle. The war went on for another three years. Most of the Jewish people ended up in concentration camps and only one per cent came back alive. Our family were all killed but we [three] survived by hiding and being helped by our friends."

Dragging my little Suitcase

Rob told this story, *"My mother once told me, perhaps as long as 40 years after the war, that when she dropped me off at my Christian hiders and left me, I tried to follow her dragging my little suitcase behind me. I was two years old. She said she could see in my eyes that I would never forgive her. I denied that because she had saved my life. What courage! She gave me up in order to give me a chance to live. But she was right. At some level deep in my soul, I never did forgive her for leaving me. Her insight was far greater than mine.*

"And I certainly cannot forgive those who forced her to make such decisions. Millions of Jewish mothers and fathers were making life and death choices, where even the wisest and luckiest ended in death for it took only one misstep, one mistake, one failure of luck, one betrayal and it was over ... ."[51]

The Munniks

Jaap said, *"*[The Munniks] *Lived in a completely different neighborhood that had nothing to do with Jewish people. It was a regular workman's neighborhood. Albert was an inspector for the waterways. He had very steady salary work. They were not poor but not rich [just working class]."*

Rob simply states, *"First of all, it was very different for the Munniks. They were able to live their lives, even with me a stranger in their home. He worked for the waterworks for the city, so he held a job, got paid however badly, I don't know. They had ration cards. He was not at risk of being picked up for slave labor because he was needed in the city."*

---

51 Krell, Robert, *Child Holocaust Survivors*, Trafford Publishing, Canada, 2007, Lecture in 2005 pg 160.

"A number of semi-independent governmental bodies, such as postal
services and employment offices, were integrated into the department
hierarchy. Only the Water Districts, special local government units
formed to maintain pumping installation for low-lying lands, were
left undisturbed, even though their offices were elective."[52]

Rob tells this story. *"In hiding with Albert, Violette Munnik, and thirteen-year-old
Nora, I was with a family of angels. I remember as clear as day the moment my father
visited me the last time to teach me I was Robbie Munnik and not to call him Dad, but
Uncle. He could no longer come, basically confined to this hiding place in his furri-
er-partner's attic."[53]

Visiting would be less frequent because of the forced labor draft around
1943 for all Dutch men between 18 and 40 years old. *"Fortunately, Albert was
too old for the forced labor draft to work in Germany. Albert was born in 1900, so
he was 42 when I came there. Nora went to school every day. It was sort of normal
in very abnormal circumstances."*

*"Life was pleasant for me. I suffered little. For the most part, I stayed inside.
Nora was pleasant and patient and taught me to read when I was four. The Munniks were loving people possessed of a deep, but not necessarily religious faith. They
never imposed on me beliefs, which could interfere with the acquisition of Judaism
and its traditions.*

*"We ate tulip bulbs and my Moeder would tell us they were potatoes because
she was ashamed to tell us there were none. My Vader on occasion brought home a
rabbit to eat [provided by Albert's brother Harry]. Vader killed it with his bicycle
pump and the carcass hung in the kitchen. I think my dad was able to funnel some
money from the business to them to help."*

*Robert Krell (then Robbie
Munnik Age 4) as a hidden
child, photographed with a
neighbor's dog. {Courtesy of
Robert Krell}.*

---

52 Warmbrunn, Werner, *The Dutch under German Occupation 1940-1945*, Stanford Press, 1963, pg 37.

53 Krell, Robert, *Child Holocaust Survivors*, Trafford Publishing, Canada, 2007, Lecture in 1997 pg 95.

Being Afraid and Silent

Rob never cried, never complained about being ill, and was very silent. He knew as an infant that his life was in danger.

Rob shares these memories, *"Outside, German soldiers marched around the square. From our front window, we could see them and sometimes V2 rockets were fired over The Hague. One looked to fall close by but it was only an illusion.*

"One day Nora took me out in the baby carriage. A German soldier approached us and 'I drew the covers over me.' He helped us through a flooded street in The Hague. Years later I asked Nora what was she doing taking me out. At first, she denied me my memory, the first response of most adults 'You were too young to remember.' Finally, she gave in to my three-year-old mind. She explained that she thought babies should see their mothers. 'I was taking you to your mother's hiding place.' She said no more. Another few years passed and I asked if we made it there. 'Yes.' replied Nora, 'and that was the day the SS came to search. We hid under the bed … .'

"My father visits. I am just over two years old. I cuddle close to him and feel the gun in his inside [my vest] pocket. Forty years later, I tell him of that moment. His response, it is not possible that I remember, and in any case, he always carried the gun in an outside pocket for easy access. Then he suddenly recalls that since he did not want it to fall out if he flung his jacket over the chair, on that day he had placed the gun inside … .

"I broke a Christmas ornament while decorating the tree. The little silver glass bugle shatters. It is of no consequence and my hiding parents are kind and gentle. My degree of upset and fear is totally out of proportion to the event. Now I know why. Will I be able to stay there? Will they allow me to stay if I break things?"[54]

---

54 Krell, Robert, *Child Holocaust Survivors*, Trafford Publishing, Canada, 2007, Lecture in 1991, pg 35.

The Risks

Leo states, *"After a few months, there were no Jews in The Hague. Sure, the Germans missed some but not many. New laws were made. Anyone who helps, hides, or collaborates with a Jew and does not turn him or her in, will be shot if and when caught. We told the Munniks this. Their reply was, 'We are not religious, but if God wills it that all of us survive then we will and you will get back your son.' We had to stay clear but still made arrangements so we could visit once a week. We had to walk more than one hour each way, watch, and hope that all was well during the past week ... .*

"Financially what the Munniks did could not be paid for at that time. Let us say that what we paid and what we gave them was only enough to get through the worst time. In this time, we looked for another place for ourselves, mainly to take the pressure off. We decided to split the Krell family three ways and Rob stayed where he was. [Emmy to find a separate place and me to stay with the Oversloots]. *What a risk they* [Munniks & Oversloots] *took."* What a terrible sacrifice for Emmy to have another person raise her son.

Leo continues, *"In total, Rob must have spent approximately 4 weeks in Opa Hol's home which brings us to the end of September, 1942. He then stayed with the Munniks until the middle of May 1945. We missed him roughly from age 2 to 5. We saw him almost weekly and our coming to visit never was a burden to them.*[55] *Mr. Munnik died in late 1973."*

Albert and Let Munnik 1971 at Rob's Wedding [K].

---

55 Robert is sure he only saw his Dad three times in 2 ½ years. But the testimonies of Leo and my Dad indicated he went once a week or at least once a month because food or money had to be given and of course to make sure Rob was alright. I am thinking that Rob did not remember many visits because they were so commonplace and nothing eventful happened to trigger his memory.

Robert describes Albert and Let

Robert describes Let and Albert. "[Albert's] *humility and simplicity belied his intelligence, his quick wit and his many talents. Wherever he went, people were irresistibly drawn to him. His humor and sparkling eyes required no translation—everyone could understand him. No one who has met him has ever forgotten him. He was a just man. To me he seemed saintly: an earthy, jovial saint who was totally open and not subject to fierce inner struggles. He did what had to be done.*

"*My Moeder* [Let] *inspired him and supported him. They complemented each other. I saw her again the summer of 1974. She missed him desperately as he would have her, had she passed away. And yet Moeder is not depressed for even now the strength of their relationship sustains her.*

"*These remarkable people felt that the war, as tragic as it was, brought them a son which is how God had meant it to be. My staying with them was viewed as an act of God and that was that. The issues of fear or danger or sacrifice simply did not exist for them. Honor this family. We will need more like them for it is not yet over.*"

Two sets of Parents

Rob said that after the war, "*They* [my parents] *were smart enough to share me. So when my parents went on vacations, I would stay with Let and Albert. With the little money they* [my parents] *were able to save, they went to Sweden to see a cousin. I am still sorting this out, how they fit into the family, for my memoirs. They went to Switzerland with your parents* [Jaap and Jel], *Paris, Italy, etc. As soon as they packed up, I packed and moved back with the Munniks. It was automatic. Then I would go to school from there by tram.*"

Oversloots and Krells are One Family

"We tired to live as normal as we could."

— Jacob (Jaap) Oversloot

Jaap tells this story, "He [Leo] was dark and I was dark [olive complexion]. He was younger than me, so I said he was my brother. I had the same suit as he had – same barber – eyeglass maker. So we could look like brother.

"*Many Jews were hidden behind walls and things like that; they had to go different ways to get food for those people. But for us, we did not hide the people away that lived with us. Everything was broken up in Holland anyway. People had to go all over Holland to find housing. Those people came to us and we acted as though he was my brother from the bombed out Rotterdam.*

"*Things were very confusing at the house in the beginning* [not even trusting family]. *When my family came in, it was my wife's brother and to her family it was my brother … .*

"*We worked long hours but when it was calm and quiet we would go out as much as possible. So on a quiet day we took those friends, Emmy and Leo, out to a quiet place with local streetcar or out by the water where we had a canoe, or played billiards (I was a very bad player). Once in a while, we went to a little place, close to Den Haag, and we had dinner outside. Otherwise, they would start looking like convicts* [without a tan]. *We tried to live as normal as we could.*"

"*We were very careful. I always walked with Mr. Krell and my wife always walked with Emmy. We made sure that there were some people between us so it would not look like the couples were together. That way if we were questioned, the women would have time to go another way.* [People would] *see two women walking, one is dark and one is light, which were best friends in the world. We did not want to bring ourselves to the attention of other people to ask, 'Who is he and who is she.'*"

I can picture both Leo and my dad walking straight with every confidence – having a attitude like they own the place wherever they went – that way no one would question them as they did their business.

Identification (ID)

Jaaps continues with, *"You needed to have identification papers. After they* [the Krells] *destroyed their identification papers, we had to find new ones that they could use. I got Leo a* 'Persoonsbewijs' *from a boy that used to work with me. The deal was that he had to lose it somewhere and I found it. Then my friend* [Leo] *had it altered with his picture so now he had a* Persoonsbewijs *but it still was not good enough to get ration cards. At first visitation of the identification* [would pass] *but their sealed thumbprints could not be changed. If they were arrested and checked, those thumbprints would not match. For street purposes, the ID was good enough. He has one and she has one. I could show you what they looked like."*

The front and back of the **Persoonsbewijs** *(Id) #27576 to Jacob Simon Oversloot issued 23 Oct 1941 as a 'Bontwerker' (Furrier) address of Miquelstraat 20 signed in 's-Gravenhage (The Hague).*

Insurance

Jaap goes into detail about, *"When the Jewish family came first in the house I bought life insurance in case something would happen to me, that my wife would get enough money to live on, because the whole deal was a matter of life and death. If the Germans ever found out what I was doing, my life would not be worth a plugged nickel."*

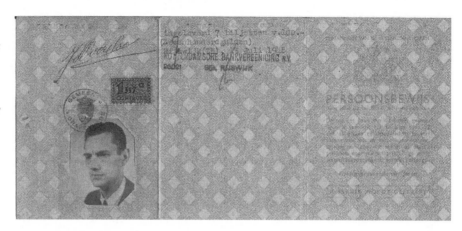

"Although legally there was no mandatory death penalty for helping Jews, 1,100...were executed for their activities."[56]

Jaap also had a bracelet made out of gold wedding rings.[57] It was four horizontal gold rings flattened together and one vertical ring made oval to attach the four horizontal rings. This was continued until it was large enough to circle Jel's wrist. If she needed to, she could break off one ring at a time for payment of food or other items. She always wore it and never took it off until after the war. It was her personal insurance policy.

"At any moment a safer area could suddenly become very dangerous; conversely, an area once thick with Germans might become relatively safe."[58]

---

56 Oliner, Samuel and Pearl, *The Altruistic Personality*, The Free Press, NY, 1988, pg 37.

57 After my mother died in 1970, my Dad had it made into a watchband for himself. It is unknown where it is today.

58 Oliner, Samuel and Pearl, *The Altruistic Personality*, The Free Press, NY, 1988, pg 123.

Emmy Krell Moves Out

"After three to six months with us," Jaap continues, *"we decided that it was better to find a room for Emmy close by, there being no more Jews* [in the city] *and everybody was taken away by the Germans. It was not as dangerous anymore to rent a room to a woman, telling her husband was in the underground."*

Rob states, *"I remember she* [Emmy] *felt that, she wanted to find a place of her own, because it was overwhelming for her to look after four children, including an infant and your mother, and not have me* [with her].

"She may have thought she was a burden on your family. It is complicated. Who could know? Obviously, her leaving did not change her affection for your family. It was not about anything held against them." By the end of 1942, *"she* [Emmy] *got false Swiss papers and documents. She found a little apartment and lived there on her own."* According to Jaap, Emmy lived in a room with a Swiss lady in 'Rijswijk' not too far from our house.

Making a living

Jaap said, *"In the beginning in 1942, work was hard to find. I was lucky, I was good friends with my former department head and he gave me some work to take home. But we needed a lot of money for all the extras we had to buy. There were no food stamps* [Ration Cards] *for the Jewish people. Food for the extra people needed to be obtained in the black market."*

"Rescuers, like nonrescuers, worried both before and during the war about feeding, sheltering, and protecting themselves and their families. What distinguished rescuers was their lack of concern with self, external approval or achievement, but rather their capacity for extensive relationships – their stronger sense of attachment to theirs and their feeling of responsibilities for the welfare of others … ."[59]

---

59 *Ibid.*, pg 249.

Johanna stated that Dad said, *"If the German soldiers had been honest, there would not have been food during the war. They traded food for gin and that is how food got to the black market."*

"The killers drank heavily. Alcohol somehow made the work more bearable."[60]

Jaap continues, *"In the meantime, the Germans were picking up Jews day and night, but there were still some Jewish people left in the key positions. Quite a few fur dealers were Jewish and most of them had stored away part of their stock to keep it out of the hands of the Germans. But they were not able to sell it. Then the money was going to the Germans anyway. So some of them knew my department head and asked him what to do.*

"Then one day, I get a call to come to the office where I worked. They needed a non-Jew to deal with the Jews that had merchandise to buy. The long and short of it was that I went to see some of the dealers that had stock. They gave me some of their stock. I brought it to the store wrote an invoice out in my name, pocket the money to give back to the dealer. My boss never used the store money but gave me some commission out of his own pocket. Well, that was fine with me."

The Partnership During the War

Jaap simply states, *"That kind of business went on for some time. After we had a bit of money, we started buying some stuff on our own and started making fur coats out of it. We decided to set up shop in the attic in my house. I had to stop working at my job and we [Leo and I] started working at a 50/50 deal starting September 1942.*[61] *We worked all we could. I had to find seamstresses outside of the house for the finishing work.*

---

60 Berenbaum, Michael, *The World Must Know,* Johns Hopkins University Press, 1993, pg 96.

61 I found letterhead paper, "J.S. Oversloot, Bontwerkerij, Miquelstraat 20, Den Haag, postgiro 299467, Bankier: Rotterdamsche Bank Ver - Rijswijk."

"The time was such that the demand for fur coats was great because of the lack of materials to make coats from wool or other materials. The sources of wool from England, Belgium, and France dried up. So we had to find ways to obtain merchandise in Holland itself. I would go to search for fur skins and so did Leo Krell. We had no trouble selling those fur coats. Leo and I made the fur coats that were to be sold at the store plus the coats we made to sell ourselves. So, we had work coming out of our ears."

"Many items such as clothing and shoes were unavailable by 1943. Varieties of substitutes were invented for such items as tea, coffee, tobacco and soap. Even these substitutes were rationed in 1943."[62]

Leo and Jaap sold fur goods to the Germans too. Rob indicated, *"That some people said that made them 'collaborators.' I say that is nonsense. That was survival. They made [fur items] so that Jaap would not be deported [to German forced labor camps]. And it made it possible to have a business on the side that could sustain the family of six and my father could earn a little bit of money and get foodstuffs for me and the Munniks too. They did what they had to do to survive."*

No Assistance was Requested or Needed

Jaap firmly said, *"We acted on our own. We needed no assistance from the underground or anyone. Because we were furriers, we had quite a bit of work. No one could buy any coats nothing was available [and the fuel to keep warm was limited]. So, we could sell left and right our fur coats. As long as we could sell fur coats, we could make all the money we wanted. And all the food we needed, what we could not buy with [Ration] coupons, we got on the black market. We never had to ask anyone for help. Not for money and not for distribution tickets [ration cards]."*

---

62 Warmbrunn, Werner, *The Dutch under German Occupation 1940-1945*, Stanford Press, 1963, pg 80.

Clothes

Jeannette recalls as time passed, *"There was no more cotton, wool or linen for clothes and towels. Oom Henk was very talented with machinery. He had motorized Mom's sewing machine before the war. Mom would make clothes from other clothes, combine sheets to make one out of two sheets that were worn, and make hand washcloths out of worn towels."*

Jenny remembers, *"Mom would take her clothes and Dad's clothes and take them completely apart. From that material, she would make clothes for the children or the other people in the house as needed. During the war, you could not get material. We were lucky Mom knew how to sew. We always had something to wear. Dad made fur coats for all the children out of scraps of fur to keep us warm. He even made me a fur blanket. They were very frugal and nothing went to waste.*

"Anything that was knitted would be taken apart and used to make new sweaters or socks from what was left over. The children helped to take the wool apart and wind it up on a spool for knitting again. Oma Oversloot did most of the knitting."

Lack of Communications

Jaap stated, *"There was little to no contact with family and friends because everyone was too busy just staying alive [after 1942]. You could not go wherever you wanted. If you had a brother, sister or mother—they were pretty much on their own. Telephones were limited and you had to write letters. If there was a gathering of people we never talked—we would go on as if we had nothing to do with it and went on with our lives."*

"Despite their hostility toward Nazis, the majority of bystanders were overcome by fear, hopelessness, and uncertainty. These feelings encourage self-centeredness and emotional distancing from others, and provided fertile soil for passivity. Survival of the self assumes paramount importance."[63]

---

63 Oliner, Samuel and Pearl, *The Altruistic Personality*, The Free Press, NY, 1988, pg 146.

Trust In Oneself

Robert told a story about his father during the war. Leo had a very bad toothache. He had an appointment to see a dentist and while walking to his appointment he passed the office and kept on walking. He decided to endure the pain. He found out later that the SS were waiting for him at the dentist office. This is an example of how they lived during the war on instincts.

A rescuer that was "carving out new relationships and roles and redefining old ones vis-a-vis the Jews in their care and neighbors and other members of the community required new skills. The basic issue was whom one could trust and whom one could not."[64]

> "Rescuers also had to deal with the occupiers, and the enemy wore more than one face. Enemies included Nazis, ordinary Germans, soldiers, indigenous collaborators, and local police … . Rescuers were constantly faced with the challenge of discerning these differences."[65]

Being Afraid

Jaap continues, *"We had a system of looking out for the Gestapo. During the day, Johanna or Jack would report to us if the Gestapo was in our neighborhood. We would watch when they were close to our front door. Oma Oversloot [or Jel] would pinch all the children and make them cry. Most of the time the soldiers would avoid our door. They did not want to go into a house with screaming children. Occasionally, that was not enough and when the Gestapo came, we just said this is my brother and after reviewing the false papers or gathering the goods they were collecting, they would leave.*

"The Krells told me later they were often afraid."

---

64 *Ibid.*, pg 101.
65 Oliner, Samuel and Pearl, *The Altruistic Personality*, The Free Press, NY, 1988, pg 80.

I can picture Leo carrying a gun for protection. After all he was previously military police and Rob does remember him having a gun when he came to visit. I just wonder if he ever had to use it. I don't believe my father ever had a gun or knew how to use it.

Jaap continues, *"We were only afraid once. One time, those people that were living at our place* [The Krells], *they had that little boy, and they would go to the people who were taking care of him to bring them money and to see the child. There was a curfew of 10 PM for everyone to be off the streets.*

"One time they were gone, it was past 10 PM, and they were not back. I could not send my wife and children away because of the curfew, so they could not go on the street. I did not know what to do. They may have been picked up by the Gestapo or something could have happened to them when they were visiting the child. Were they hiding somewhere? Everybody was in a panic. The foster parents did not have a phone – I did not know their address[66] *– Everything had to wait until the next morning. It was a messy situation.*

"Then after few hours, they showed up. The only reason they were late was because they could not get through because there was a fire somewhere which they had to walk-around. I was raving mad at them, but they were not at fault. Then I was glad they were back safe. We imagined the worst for a few hours and then it was over."

Were the Children Afraid?

Johanna and Jack remember, *"When a neighbor came out, stood on the stairway, and pointed a gun at us. He said 'if you guys don't go inside, I am going to shoot you.' That scared us and, for a while, we stayed inside."* After the war, it was discovered that this neighbor was a traitor.

---

66 Jaap did not want to know that information in order to keep the Munnik safe in case he was picked up by the Germans.

Jack said, *"During the war you did not have friends, you did not talk to anybody, you could not associate with anyone, you could not have friends or let them know what you were doing. It is like being in your own little jail cell. People who talked got into trouble. If you don't talk, you can't get into trouble because nobody knows."*

"Life became even more family-centered than before the war. Blackout and curfew kept people at home. Travel became more difficult since tires wore out and bicycles were hidden, trains were overcrowded, and streetcars did not run after dark."[67]

Sirens

Jeannette said, *"I heard the rocket shot off by my school. They wanted to hit London. They made a lot of noise. Before and after school I would hear sirens and would have to find a stairway to hide to protect myself from bombs. German bombs would miss a train station and people were killed, homes demolished especially in certain neighborhoods.*

"We had a lot of sirens go off and blackouts. At home when the sirens went off in the middle of the night, we would go down to the landing until the all clear siren went on."

Johanna remembers, *"Being sent to the library to pick up and return books. When I was about 8 or 9 [1944-1945], I was almost to the library when the sirens went off, and I laid near a building for protection. The bomb I was hiding from went straight through that staircase next to the Library. I turned around and went home."*

Jenny said, *"The airplanes made a lot of noise. Even with my bad hearing, I could hear them. Backfires of cars still scare me today."*

---

67 Warmbrunn, Werner, *The Dutch under German Occupation 1940-1945*, Stanford Press, 1963, pg 100.

Jack said, *"I was protected because I was so young. The war started when I was 2 years old and ended when I was 7 years old. We were pretty restricted where and what we could do during the war but it opened up after the war."*

Access to Food

"The average daily ration for adults from 1941 to the summer of 1944 was about half the average prewar consumption in terms of calories. It dropped by only 15 percent during this period. The average ration of between 1,500 and 2,000 calories, usually augmented by food secured outside of rationing channels, did not represent a famine level, but it led to the progressive weakening of human energy and resistance to disease. ... In August 1943, rationing of fruits and vegetables began and 95 percent of the diet had come under rationing regulations."[68]

Jeannette remembers, *"Mom and Emmy used Food Stamps* [Ration Cards] *to get food such as potatoes, tulip bulbs, bread, etc. You were allowed one loaf of bread per person per week. It never was enough. It was supplemented with the goods bought on the black market.*

"We had many meals at lunchtime. The big fish they had cooked and the eyeballs were still there. We mostly ate beans—all kinds of beans." That is why Jeannette and Johanna still do not like them today.

Johanna remembers, *"The oats were raw and had to be milled, which we did with a little coffee grinder. There was no milk, no sugar to cook with oats, but we ate better than the rest of the city. In the beginning of all this, people used to steal our potato peels and everything else that they could eat out of our garbage pail."*

Jenny remembers one funny story about having a single orange. *"Mom did not know what she was going to do with the one orange. There were always so many people to feed at the house – so she squashed it in the green beans with the pulp."*

---

68 *Ibid.*, pg 79.

> "Material shortages also made housekeeping difficult, since shopping took more time and available goods were of poor quality. Meal planning required more effort and ingenuity. Soap and other household items became scarce, as did luxury items such as tobacco and alcohol."[69]

Jeannette indicated Mom said, *"Dad stopped smoking during the war, it was just too expensive."*

Cooking/Heat Resources

Johanna recalls, *"No one had any way to cook anything as the war progressed. There was no gas or electricity. You were lucky if you had wood burning fireplaces, although there wasn't any wood to burn. All the trees were chopped down and all wooden gates were taken. People had to resort to chopping up the pavement and use the tar to burn. So the streets were in sad shape to say the least."*

Jaap told this story, *"He had a neighbor who first burned his books, than the shelves and bookcase, door frames, furniture and any wood in the house that was not needed. The house was gutted by the end of the war.*

> "Meanwhile, the official fuel [gas] ration dropped [in 1944] to approximately one-third of that of 1940-41, and most families received only a fraction of their official allocation. In desperation, people in the cities cut down trees in parks and streets, tore out streetcar ties, wrecked abandoned houses, such as those vacated by deported Jews, and stole any wood they could find. During this period, nearly all the energy of the urban population went to securing food and fuel to ensure physical survival."[70]

---

69 *Ibid.*, pg 100.
70 Berenbaum, Michael, *The World Must Know*, Johns Hopkins University Press, 1993, pg 100.

Jan [my mother's nephew and son of brother Jan] and his brother Kees, ages 9 and 13, respectively, remember this during the war, *"They went to a place in their neighborhood near the railway line. The trains went very slow there. They would climb on board the train and throw coal on the ground. Later, they would pick up the coal and take it home for the family to use."*[71]

Jan Steiger age 9 [Courtesy o Tessy Steiger}.

Helping Others

Jeannette remembers, *"Mom used to feed the kids next door on alternate weeks and give them a plate of food to take home."*

Jenny remembers, *"Mom and Dad would feed many neighbors. It was so hard to get food during the war. There was a family with many little children and Mom knew that they had not eaten for days. The family was picked up by the Germans. She was very angry and without thought to her safety, she went to the Germans with food and told them they needed to feed this family. She always thought about other people first. She realized the risk later. The family never came back. They may have been Jewish or helping the Jews.*

"Mom was like that, she would give to everyone before herself. That was her strength and courage. That was her nature. She wanted to always be good to others."

Famine

"... After September 1944, rationing was carried out on the local level. The size of rations was related directly to the quantity of supplies at hand. Therefore, rationing conditions varied widely from one region to another … . The heavily populated section of the western seaboard, especially the big cities, suffered most during the final winter of the war.

---

71 Information and photos are from 2010 letters from Thessy Steiger, who lives in Best, Netherlands. The letter was translated from Dutch to English by a computer program on "Word."

"During the famine winter of 1944-1945, public food services set up in 1940 for assisting needy persons assumed great importance in supporting the city population of Western Holland. In Amsterdam, they served 300,000 people, or nearly 40 percent of the total population, during the peak of operations in May 1945. During the last weeks of the Occupation, when the rations dropped below 500 calories in the big cities, supplies donated and shipped by the Swiss and Swedish Red Cross were distributed free through regular rationing channels. Despite these efforts, the general health of the population in the cities of the Western Netherlands deteriorated after October 1944, and serious illness and death from starvation occurred among people in institutions and among the old and the very poor."[72]

Black Market During the Famine

As the family story goes, Jaap once paid 60 guilders [like 60 U.S. dollars] for one egg when the youngest child would not eat.

"Despite the vigorous attempts of the German and Dutch administrations, many consumer goods found their way into the black market, which served German as well as Dutch customers. During the final winter of the war, reliance on the black market became a necessity for the urban population. During this period, black-market prices rose to extraordinary heights, sometime to more than one hundred times the official rate, and frequently a barter arrangement had to be made instead of payment in cash."[73]

---

72 Warmbrunn, Werner, *The Dutch under German Occupation 1940-1945*, Stanford Press, 1963, pg 79-80.
73 *Ibid.*, pgs 81.

Trading Goods

As the famine progressed, other resources had to be tapped. The black market was too expensive and had a little food. Jaap used to take a bicycle without tires to a farm and take a fur coat to trade for a 50-pound bag of beans. He then traded half the beans for wood that Jack would cut the wood into small pieces for cooking. Jaap recalls being more afraid for his life caring a large bag of beans or potatoes home than obtaining it.

Jeannette stated Dad said, *"We ate a fur coat a week."*

> "In the final months before [German] surrender, the people of the cities of Western Holland, especially children, women, and old men scoured the countryside in an effort to barter with farmers for food. Some expeditions in search of food for the family took as long as two weeks."[74]

Jeannette said, *"Sometime during the summer or fall of 1944, I heard people talk about American soldiers landing and we would be free soon but that did not happen until May 5, 1945. Dad said, it was good the war ended so we could get food from the American Red Cross. The food came like in big barrels and we had to bring a plate or dish to put the food on. Dad said, all of us would have died if the war had gone on longer, because there was no food available even on the black market … . There was no food to be found anywhere for any price."*

---

74 *Ibid.*, pg 80.

"The death rate increased substantially in 1944 and early 1945, owing to the cumulative effect of undernourishment and the frequency of contagious disease. In Amsterdam, so many people died that it became impossible to bury all corpses promptly, in view of the lack of transportation and coffins. As a result of the famine of 1944-45, approximately 15,000 persons succumbed in the northwestern part of The Netherlands alone. The total number of deaths in 1945 was nearly twice that of 1939."[75]

Bike ride with Dad

Rob told this story, *"I remember, one of the few times I got to go out. I must have been close to 5 years old* [maybe early 1945], *after the hunger winter when everyone was starving. I went on a bike with my Vader* [Leo] *and we rode into the flat farmland, maybe Zeeland or something. I know we came back with fruit, vegetables, strawberry jam, cheese and stuff like that. Somehow, there was enough money. Somehow, we went out and for some reason he took me, which was probably a risky thing to do. I enjoyed the trip on the back of the bike."*

---

75 *Ibid.*, pgs 102-103.

More Siblings Memories of WWII

"Households with children posed a particular threat. Children were more likely to reveal secrets; adults who might be willing to risk their own lives and the lives of other adults would be less willing to jeopardize unknowing children. Yet 27 percent of the rescuers lived in a household with at least one child aged ten years or younger."[76]
– Samuel and Pearl Oliner

Jaap said, "Jeannette, Johanna, Jack and Jenny were not old enough to know that Tante Emmy and Oom Leo were Jews. They did not know what a 'Jew' was. If there were visitors, they were family – simple. As for the children, they never knew."

Children's memories revealed. These are vignettes by subject from interviews with my siblings.

Remembering Emmy and Leo

Jack remembers, *"Tante Emmy and Oom Leo lived in the attic. Dad, Leo and Mom working on the furs but not Emmy."*

Jeannette remembers, *"The one male worker stretched the furs and did prep work before the furs could be sewed together.*

"Besides the outside seamstress, a male about 19 years old came to work every day. Jel fed him lunch. He was the go-between [to get the furs, thread] and bring them to the attic. Jenny does not recall seeing him after the war."

Jenny stated, *"Emmy and Leo never picked me up but they would talk to me. I was ill during that time and they did not want to get too close because they might pass it on to Rob when they went to visit him. They were always nice to me. They were just there; they were part of the family. I never knew different."*

---

76 Oliner, Samuel and Pearl, *The Altruistic Personality*, The Free Press, NY, 1988, pgs 125-126.

A Place to Hide

Jeannette said that at the beginning of the war, *"They made a basement access from a cabinet in the kitchen to our small back yard. There was a pile of coal there on the outside backyard to make a fire in the stove to heat food and water."*

Jack remembers, *"A cellar where Dad used to keep carrots. The exit was the back porch where I chopped wood."*

Johanna remembers, *"Tante Hil and grandma Oversloot ("Oma") stayed with us. Johanna believed Oma Oversloot came to live with us after Oom Henk Oversloot was picked up by the Germany for forced labor [after 1943]. That is when Leo, Dad, and the apprentice would hide in the basement from time to time. That is where they stored potatoes, carrots and apples at the beginning of the war. The entrance to the basement was through the floor of a closet in the kitchen."*

Jenny said later, *"After the war, Mom had her chickens outside by the hole, the laundry and clothesline."*

Angry Dad

I remember a story that goes like this. *"One time the Germans picked up one of my dad's workers. It could have been a seamstress that did outside work for my father. My father was enraged and marched right up to the detention area, into the General's office on the third floor and demanded the worker be returned to him. The General was so stunned that my father was not stopped by any soldiers before arriving at his office on the third floor that he released the worker. That was very unusual for my dad. No fear, just anger.*

"I can picture my dad, walking straight and tall [he was 6' 2'] in his expensive double-breasted-suit walking in the detention headquarters as if he owned the place with his head held high. Then reading signs walked right into the General's office and demanded in a very forceful but gentlemanly way to return his worker.

"This had to be after 1942, but before 1943, when Dutchmen between the ages of eighteen and forty were forced to provide labor services in Germany."

Angry Jeannette

Jeannette tells this funny story, *"One day I was sent to my room and I don't remember why but I was mad at Mom. My mom stored chocolate bars in my closet and I ate them all to punish Mom. I also used to go to the basement and get the food we needed to set the table or whatever. I found the strawberry jam and I had a good time eating some of that."*

School

Jeannette continues with this cute story, *"School was real cold during the fall, winter and part of spring. Dad made us all fur coats. I did not like to wear my leopard skin coat. Sometimes we were naughty and stole thin writing books from the teachers."*

"In some ways, children and teenagers were less affected by the Occupation than were adults. Most schools continued as usual until the winter of 1944-45, and many young people were able to carry on their customary youth activities in church or athletic organizations. Even groups such as the Boy Scouts, which had been dissolved by Occupation authorities, continued to meet informally. On the other hand, many youngsters from urban low-income families became victims of wartime demoralization, especially if their fathers worked in Germany."[77]

Jeannette stated, *"One of my middle school teachers was a resistance fighter. He helped the Jews by doing the legwork to fight the Nazis towards the end of the war."*

"On the whole, Nazi authorities met with little success in their attempt to Nazify teaching personnel. Until the Liberation in 1945, the majority of teachers remained loyal patriots, although higher administrative echelons were staffed with collaborators."[78]

---

77 Warmbrunn, Werner, *The Dutch under German Occupation 1940-1945*, Stanford Press, 1963, pgs 100-101.
78 *Ibid.*, pg 47.

Jeannette remembers Jenny

Jeannette talks about mom, *"I never knew my mother was pregnant. One time I asked where babies came from and she said, 'The cabbage patch.' That generation of parents did not talk about sex. Most families had four or more children. There was no birth control at that time. I know that we had no Kotex then. They had to use used towels and soak them in salt water before washing them for reuse.*

"Jenny was born January 1940, stayed in Mom's bedroom because she was always sick. Oma and Mom took care of her. I know Mom got really mad when Jenny took one hour or more to eat and then threw up. One time they tried not feeding her and she gained a pound.

"When Jenny managed to get diphtheria and we had to walk to the hospital [there were no trams available]. I had to take Jack and Johanna with me. I do not know if Mom was with us but she must have been since I was probably seven or eight years old, Johanna five years old, and Jack three years old at the time. We also stayed with friends when Mom and Jenny came down with the measles."

"To many people in the occupied territory, declining health conditions presented an additional worry. The incidence of contagious diseases and the fatalities resulting from them increased throughout the war. In 1943, an epidemic of poliomyelitis swept the country; Tuberculosis became more prevalent despite an expanded x-ray program. In 1944, diphtheria caused many deaths, since a virulent variety of the disease had been introduced from Germany."[79]

---

79 *Ibid.*, pg 102.

Jenny's Health

Jenny told these stories, *"I was sick during the war. Fever, diphtheria, viruses, measles, chicken pox, mumps, stomach problems and could not keep food down especially milk. One of the first women doctors in The Netherlands took care of me at home. However, she brought illness with her when seeing me. Doctors did not take precautions with gowns and gloves to prevent the spreading of illnesses. The doctor just washed her hands.*

"Daddy, in a small wine glass, mixed a raw egg with sugar in it with some berry juice [gooseberry or raspberry], a type of syrup and it was one of a few things I would keep down. Mom stated 'That everyone had cod liver oil each morning and we fought over who would get the first spoonful.'

"I have a hearing problem that Mom said 'Was caused by a double ear infection. They used warm oil in my ear. They tried to do surgery but there was no anesthetic, so they held me down.' Dad said, 'I had more strength than an adult' when they held me down. They punctured the eardrum on the left and were able to drain the ear on the right a little. My hearing is 50% in the right ear that is now down to 40%. I have no hearing in the left ear.

"They would try to bring me downstairs to get me to eat, but the moment I saw food I would scream bloody murder like someone was trying to feed me poison. I did not want to see food, smell food, or eat food. Jeannette always said, 'I screamed [not cried] a lot.'

"Oma was always in my room to comfort me, hold me, or Oma sat there knitting. Mom had to change all the clothes and the linen to ensure the other children did not get sick too. There was always cleaning and washing. And later it was hard to get soap.

"Mom said when I was between 3-5 years old; she was extremely upset one time trying to get me to eat. She dropped everything, went to the doctor and said 'you think it is so easy to feed her you try it.' The doctor laughed and thought it was funny and he tried to feed me and he could not. The doctor said, 'here,' to the nurse, 'you feed her.' Mom's reply was, 'I have three other children at home to feed and can't spend all day with Jenny.' So Jenny was put in the hospital for a while.

"Mom said the hospital did not want me anymore because it was so hard to feed me and they did not have the patience. Finally the doctor said to give me spicy food. Indonesian food would stay down. So spicy food kept me going."

Johanna and Jeannette c. 1936.

Jeannette's Eye Sight

In 1936, at the age of two, and again at age 12, Jeannette had operations to correct her vision. That is why most childhood pictures of Jeannette have her one eye not focused.

Jeanette states that, *"After the operation, my eyes worked independently and as a result, my depth perception was always off. In addition, I had pneumonia when I was ten and I had to have a lot of juice to get better. It took about six weeks to get better. There was no medicine available in 1944. This may be why my lungs have very low capacity and why I did not like sports. I was always happy reading books."*

"The new emphasis on home life caused an increase in the sale of books, until 1942 the paper shortage forced a reduction of publications. Historical and travel literature and textbooks were much in demand."[80]

I Spy - Johanna

Johanna's story goes like this: *"During 1944 and 1945, when I was 8 years old, soldiers came to the house to pick up any males from 18-40 years old. The males were sent by train to Germany as laborers or to work for the German Army in the factories. After the deadline, if they saw any man, they would arrest them, line them up against a wall and shoot them.[81] During that time, it was very dangerous for Dad and Leo, so I was lookout to see where the soldiers were congregated.*

---

80 *Ibid.*, pg 100.
81 Johanna may have experienced this in person.

"I was alert to too many things. They would send me to the corner
to see where the German soldiers were hanging out. They were mainly
at the cigar store at the corner or the bar across the street. Even though
Jeannette was older, I was sent because Jeanette was not alert enough and
could get distracted easily.

"From time to time, Leo, Dad, and the apprentice would hide in the
basement. The entrance to the basement was through the floor of a closet
in the kitchen. The only air that was down there was from the sewer pipe
that went to the backyard."

*"The workshop is in the sitting room—
very cozy."*

Twelve and a half Anniversary Party

Jaap and Jel were married 29 July 1931. It was the custom to have a
12½-anniversary party. The menu consisted of chicken soup, pastry shell with
fish, potatoes and vegetables, compote with cooked pears, cheese and coffee.

Jeannette fondly remembers the large party with all their friends and
relatives in attendance.

"Hil and my mom saved up Ration Cards for months for this 'weekend
long party' starting Saturday, 29 January 1944.

"I had to go to the bakery to pick up the cake. I tripped over a metal
corner curb with the cake in my hands. The cake was smashed. The par-
tygoers ate it anyway. The children watched slides with my brother's new
toy. We swung the swing on the stairs toward the front door. Five or more
of the children slept in a full bed sideways for the weekend."

Dad took art drawing and painting classes during the beginning of the war.
So, one of the unusual features of the party was that my father drew a different
picture, on the front of each menu, with colored pencils.[82]

The Copper Wedding Table "ATTACK!"

---

82 Jenny has the original menus with the drawings on the front and Willy deSwaaf-
Robson translated the sayings from Dutch to English.

The pictures depicted their courtship and married life. You can also get an idea of Dad's dry sense of humor.

Here are some of the drawings with the English translation:

"Jel with dinner for Jaap."

"Moving – First salt to bring good luck."

"We are going to clean— What about that?"

"Jel in her domain – She loves cooking and does it so well"

"Wonderful holiday with beautiful weather."

"An accident – I could cry."

"The journey to Haarlem with excellent weather."

"Some things made for the bottom drawer" (underwear)

After the War

"Lots of joy for the Dutch people, especially the Jewish people, but no food for all those people."
– Jacob (Jaap) Oversloot

T he day before liberation in The Hague, Rob remembers, "On May 5, 1945, I don't know why they did this, I guess they just couldn't wait, Moeder and Vader (Let and Albert) took me to my mother's hiding place (and it could have been May 4 or 5) but it was still early because I actually looked out the front window and saw Canadian halftracks chasing German halftracks.

"*Those bastards were still shooting. They gunned down the guy across the street that kept peeking out of the door. And I saw that.* [I was four almost five years old at the time]. *I saw him shot and then they pulled me back from the window. But my legs* [would not move]. *But I had just seen this. The transports were just turning on the street. They were shooting from their halftracks. You can imagine they were fleeing in defeat being chased by the Canadian Army of all things.*

"*They were gunning people down on the street. I always thought about that because they got so close to making it you know.*"

Germans Leave

Jaap said, "*Finally, the war was over. The Germans went home with whatever they had, carrying their stuff in stolen baby strollers, pushcarts, and bicycles. Lots of joy for the Dutch people, especially the Jewish people, but no food for all those people.*

"*We just had to make do with the rest of the food we had until the old govern- ment started dropping food by airplane. No trains, no autos and the main bridges were blown up. It must have taken three months before there was any food to speak of.*

"But we made it. Everybody was still alive: the little Jewish boy, Robert, by that time 5 years old, his father, his mother, the boy who did not go to Germany [my helper], my wife and children, and so was I."

Leo, Robert and Emmy about 1946

Victory in Europe Day

Rob remembers, *"VE Day I remember well. Crowds celebrated in the streets and British planes dropped food parcels. White bread was considered the greatest treat."*

The Peperzak

In hope that the Krells could put their lives back together, Jaap states, *"I put my partner in contact with a man and wife that had been on the wrong side of the war and still not found out, but could no longer be free. There was no place to go for him but he had an apartment above an empty store that used to be a fur store. He sold us the store, lock stock and barrel, for 2000 guilders. So my partner had shop on the first floor, an apartment on the second floor,[83] and a workroom on the third floor. Everything needed for living with his wife and child as a family after those very bad years."*

"In 1945 when the war was over, we were furriers making fur coats. Me and him were still partners 50/50. We had a shop, made and sold fur coats retail. We had a going fur business during that time."

The business was named the 'Peperzak' and as of 2008, there was still a small sign on the side of the building to that effect.

---

83 Robert remembers the apartment. I slept beside the dining room table and my parents used the one bedroom.

Rob recalls, *"Jaap made coats in the atelier on the third floor and with some help; she [Emmy] sold them downstairs in the store. She was a super saleslady. All the aristocrats of Europe came to the store to buy fur coats. And movie stars too."*

Traitors

Jeannette said, *"After the war, the Dutch government had a trial for all the traitors. If you were found to be a traitor, they shaved your head and paraded you around the city. We found out that some traitors lived on our street. One as close as where the Germans took the cars [that was across the street]. Another lived on the other side of the block right by the corner where kids played. Anyway, they had been all around us and we made it through the war. We were lucky."*

The Peperzak – 149 Spui, Den Haag and the sign still on the side of the building, 2008.

"Most rescuers perceived their neighbors as threatening. Frequently, the threat was very real."[84]

Leo and Emmy's Health

Rob tells this story about his parents health. *"Leo had jaundice from all the stuff and hunger at the end of the war. My mother [Emmy] had all kinds of stomach problems her whole life. She was a strong-willed woman but eating bad things or not eating at all shrinks your stomach and it affects your whole being. They were not in good shape in 1945."*

---

84 Oliner, Samuel and Pearl, *The Altruistic Personality,* The Free Press, NY, 1988, pg 124.

Family Reunion

Rob continues, *"At age five, after three years in the home of Mr. and Mrs. Munnik and my sister Nora, I thought I was theirs. They loved me so much. Years later, I asked my Christian mother, had she wanted my parents to die? In her usual no-nonsense, truthful manner 'it crossed my mind, you would have been my son. But for your sake, I wanted your parents to live.'"*

Rob was devastated to be taken away from his Moeder, Vader and Nora at the end of the war. "Nora was not allowed to see me for a couple of weeks so that I could get used to my folks again. Well those two weeks were my worst, really, and it was her worst. Poor Nora missed me terribly. Her interpretation of Holocaust trauma was not all the people who were murdered, but the loss of her little brother and my loss of her. But then we always kept in touch."

Looking for Family

Jaap states, *"Later some of the people came back from Germany out of the concentration camps. It took years and years to get them in human shape again. Some never did. Emmy and Leo worked with the survivors in hopes of finding their family [mothers, fathers, and siblings] but mostly to no avail."*

Rob remembers, *"My father and I drove in a truck to Groningen [last North-east Province of The Netherlands] and picked up dozens of Jewish children from their hiding places on farms. I learned only later that most were orphans and that some ended up in orphanages and others were taken by the Bricha to Palestine."* [85]

Map of The Netherlands and its Provinces locations. Groningen is in the upper right hand corner. {Wiki/Netherlands}.

"Immediately after the war, rescuers and nonrescuers alike were most concerned about restoring some normalcy to their lives. Rescuers and rescued who were together until the war's end generally parted immediately or shortly thereafter. Jews went searching for kin who might have survived; surviving

---

85 Robert Krell, *Child Holocaust Survivors*, Trafford Publishing, 2007, Lecture in 2000 pg 123.

parents or other family members came back to reclaim their children ... . The vast majority of (rescuers), however, remained where they were and turned their attention to themselves and their own families. The dominant concern of all was the reconstruction of shattered lives. Above all, they had to attend to their own wounds, physical and psychological, as well as those of family members."[86]

Nallie & Millie

Rob continues, *"When I came out of hiding in 1945, my constricted view of the world expanded rapidly with the discovery of other children. Second cousin Millie, age 8, had found refuge in Switzerland. First cousin Nallie, age 7, was found by my father who rode his bicycle up and down the streets of The Hague, searching for him. He [Leo] had not known what his sister Manya had done with her son before she was deported and murdered in Sobibor."* [87]

Leo went to court so Nallie could stay in Holland, as he requested, with his foster family, the Groots. Robert said, *"We saw Nallie every other Sunday after that."*

Aware of Reduced Family Size[88]

Rob continues, *"What had not occurred to me yet at the age of five and six was that I had no grandparents, aunts, or uncles. I had only Millie. Not all the stories I had heard had made much sense to me. But gradually awareness came. Everyone was dead. My parents between them had three sisters and two brothers. All gone. My paternal grandfather was deported to his death from Antwerp in August 1942."*

Emmy and Leo both discovered they were orphans – all their family had been murdered except for Nallie and Emmy's cousin Isaac's daughter, Millie. Only a few

---

86 Oliner, Samuel and Pearl, *The Altruistic Personality*, The Free Press, NY, 1988, pgs 223-224.
87 *Ibid.*, pg 123.
88 *Ibid.*, pg 97.

Jewish families survived and they were grateful to have their unit intact, as husband, wife and child.

It was a MIRACLE! Robert, Nallie and Millie were part of the lucky 7% of the Jewish <u>European</u> children who survived.

Returning Survivors

Robert sadly remembers, *"It was in 1945 that I heard the stories of those who returned, the stories that were forever engraved on my heart and mind. Millie, the 8-year old linguist, translated for me the stories no child should ever hear as we listened silently to the survivors, pretending not to understand. Even then, as a child, I became the repository of memories.*

"I was now about 5 ½ and we lived at the Spuistraat 149. Our living room became a sort of reception centre for the remnants of The Hague Jewry. Each day I saw people in such despair and heard stories so frightening that I have never forgotten them. I listened pretending not to understand either the language or the content. The adults spoke in front of us children because they thought their words and experiences were not understood.

"I saw the still fresh marks of whiplashes on the backs of friends of my parents. I saw persons who returned and were insane from their experiences. I witnessed the tearful reunions of relatives who thought the other dead. It was a most peculiar world in which to be a child. And with the years, the memories have not faded. They have grown stronger. We child survivors are but a small fragment of the first generation, finally finding a voice ... ."[89]

Precious Photographs

Around 1947 Emmy and Leo found someone left a photo album of the Krell family in the store. The anonymous person gave the Krells the precious past they so longed for.

---

89 *Ibid.*, pgs 23-24.

In 1942, they had left family history photographs behind in order to be safe in their new lives as non-Jews. If it were not for this gift, most of the Krells family pictures would have been lost and not included this book. Rob indicated a miracle occurred that day.

Visas and Immigration

Both families applied for visas to come to America around 1946. They had to wait for a quota number. Emmy and Leo got their quota number in 1950 and gave it to my father in gratitude. The Oversloots came to Pasadena, California in America October 1950. Doctors indicated we needed to get to a warm climate otherwise Jenny would not live pass the age of 12. In March 1951, the Krells immigrated to Vancouver, Canada. The quota in Canada was more relaxed and a visa for the Krells was received within a year.

Pasadena Star News April 8, 1951

Favorite and Least Favorite Memory

What is your favorite memory of being in Holland? I asked Rob.

"That is a good question. It would probably be Millie, Nallie, and I just hanging out on the beach in Scheveningen.

"My least favorite memory is walking around in The Hague in Holland with my dad as he pointed out, 'This is where your grandmother lived. This is where our friend lived,' etc. Death was all around us. It was a city of ghosts, of everyone who had lived there and been part of the youth organization and soccer club. They were all killed. There were 20,000 Jews reduced to 1,300 [in The Hague]. There were over 18,000 deaths just in that small community [The Hague]. I wanted to get out of there so bad."

Rob Visit to Holland in 1961

Rob tells this story. *"In 1961, I came to visit my Christian angels, Violette and Albert Munnik and my 'sister' Nora. I knocked on the door one flight up at Loenenschestraat 147 and the neighbor opened his door. 'Robbie?' he asked "Here to see your Moeder?'*

'Yes, meneer de Vries' replied Robert.

'Robbie, I've always meant to ask you why you never thanked me for not betraying you.'

"So, from ages 2-5, I had lived next door to death, a neighbor with the thought of betrayal in mind. Fortunately, he did not act on it. Thousands of Dutch men and women did. And Jews and neighbors died because of them."[90]

Robert, Jacob (Jaap), Leo, Emmy, Jeltje, Albert and Let Munnik at Rob's graduation from UBC -1965. [also see back cover]

Robert's life in Canada

Robert remembers, *"In 1965 I graduated in Medicine from the University of British Columbia at Vancouver. My parents arranged for Moeder and Vader to be present. It was their first trip to a foreign land.*

"Their second trip was in 1971 when I married in Vancouver. It was a unique event. My wife's parent and my two sets of parents were all there. My brother Ron (born in Canada in 1956) was best man. Moeder delivered a spontaneous speech to the 400 guests and I translated. Most guests were Jewish and many were themselves survivors. It was a happy, yet tearful event.

"Vader was already ill at that time. He had difficulty swallowing and had a choking cough. He was briefly hospitalized in Vancouver and then returned to Holland. Vader died several months later."

Leo simply stated, *"Mr. Munnik died in late 1973. We lost a good friend. Rob lost a father."*

---

90 Robert Krell, *Child Holocaust Survivors*, Trafford Publishing, Canada, 2007, Lecture in 2005 pgs 160-161.

The Yad Vashem Medal

"If I am going to die, it is going to be for the right reason,"
— **Jacob (Jaap) Oversloot [1976]**

Decency and Luck is the key to survival. But after the war, **silence** was the key. Get on with your life and forget about the past. The present is what we need to think about today.

> "The willingness of some survivors to share their stories is a recent phenomenon. For a long time, most refused to talk about the war, chiefly because the act of remembering an offense is itself traumatic. There was a lot of unresolved mourning for family members they hoped to meet again but knew deep down they never would."[91]

What triggered Jaap to start talking about the war and life in Holland was when he received the *Yad Vashem* Medal.

> "This medal that is being granted to the 'righteous' [Gentiles who saved Jews at the risk of their lives] was struck especially for *Yad Vashem* by the Israel Government Coins and Medals' Corporation. The designer Nathan Karp of Jerusalem has given both artistic and symbolical expression to the Talmudic saying: 'He who saves a single being saves a whole world.'[92] The two hands grasping a lifeline of twisted barbed wire

Yad Vashem medal to Jeltje and Jacob Oversloot.

---

91 Continuation of *The Holocaust and History: Introduction to the Survivors' Stories* by Lawrence N Powell, Tulane University – http://www.holocaustsurvivors.org/data.show.php?di=record&da=texts&ke=6.

92 Another version is "Whosoever saves a single life, saves an entire universe." Source is Michnah, Sanhedrin (4:5) www.yadvashem.org/yv/en/righteous/index.asp.

seem to reach out from the void, while the lifeline wound around the globe and giving it its impetus, proclaims that deeds such as those of the Righteous justify the world's existence and our faith in humanity."[93]

Yad Vashem Memorial Authority

"*Yad Vashem* is a memorial authority in Jerusalem established by the Holocaust Martyrs' and Heroes' Remembrance Law adopted by the Israeli Knesset (Parliament) on August 19, 1953. Its purpose is to commemorate the six million Jews [1.5 million were children], who died at the hands of the Nazis and their collaborators as well as the 'Righteous among the Nations' who risked their lives to save Jews.

"In fulfillment of the latter purpose a commission of eighteen members, composed of the chairmen of the *Yad Vashem* Directory and his deputy as well as representatives of assorted other groups and public figures, is appointed to decide who should be so designated. The commission studies all requests for recognition based on evidence provided by survivors as well as other documentary evidence. Each individual member of the commission is assigned a specific case and makes an initial recommendation.

"The member meets with at least one of the survivors in order to get a firsthand impression of the story. If there are no living survivors or if none can be met in person, a written notarized deposition by relatives or friends is acceptable. In making its final decision, the commission considers all circumstances related to the rescue story as well as the rescuer's motivation, personal risk, and dedication. The criteria for recognition by *Yad Vashem* includes (1) the rescuer was motivated by humanitarian consideration alone (2) the rescuer risked his or her own life and (3) no remuneration of any kind accompanied the rescue act."[94]

---

93 Document that came with the medal. It is in Yiddish with a French and English translation.
94 Oliner, Samuel and Pearl, *The Altruistic Personality,* The Free Press, NY, 1988, pg 262.

The *Yad Vashem* Medal Process

This award for my parents was started by the "Hidden Child," Robert (Rob) Krell. A letter from Leo to my parents, dated March 11, 1976, tells how the process was started.

"... Rob left with his family January 1975 to Jerusalem, we were there in the end of March. Rob found out about honoring the people who helped to save lives but he was too young to remember details, so all was set up that when we came, we had to fill in the details. Once you start writing a story like that, it seems that you write a book. Anyway, I managed, got the story on paper and the people in Yad Vashem were very impressed with the whole thing. From there, it is a matter of time to process the whole thing and then you are on the road ... ."

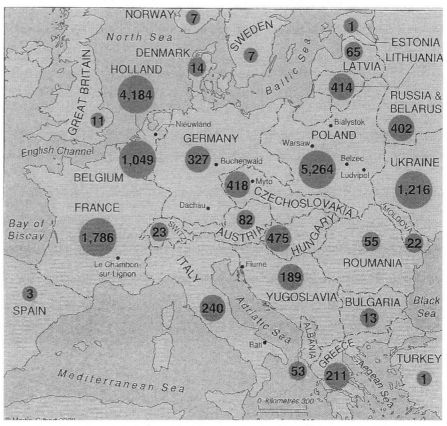

The map shows the number of people who received Yad Vashem awards per country between 1953 and 1999. {NA pg 105 Courtesy of Martin Gilbert}

Map of *Yad Vashem* Medal awarded to Righteous Gentiles [95]

Jeltje and Jacob Oversloot, Let and Albert Munnik, and Nora Munnik were part of the 4,184 recipients from The Netherlands as indicated in the map above.

---

95 Gilbert, Martin, *Never Again: A History of the Holocaust*, New York, NY, pg 105.

Julia and Charlotte's (daughter) Trip to Jerusalem 28 October 2013 - Yad Vashem Holocaust Memorial - Garden of the Righteous Netherlands.

Enlargement of inscription Oversloot Jacob & Jeltje

Letter from *Yad Vashem*

This correspondence is about the medal, "Jerusalem 29 February 1976 from Yad Vashem, Martyrs' and Hero's' Remembrance Authority Jerusalem by Doctor Moshe Beaky, President of the Commission for the Just." The body of the letter reads as follows:

"I have the honor to inform you that the Commission for Designation of the Just of Yad Vashem decided, after due deliberation, to bestow upon you and your wife Jeltje, the Medal of the Just, for the bravery and human kindness you both showed, in risking your lives in order to save Jewish lives during the Holocaust.

The Medal will be presented to you by our Consulate in Los Angeles.

You will be notified of the exact date of the presentation of the medal in the near future.

Please accept our best wishes and our gratitude."

Jaap's response is dated March 9, 1976 and reads as follows:

"This is to acknowledge your letter of February 29th from Jerusalem. Everything you speak of happened thirty-five years ago, and revived in my mind and heart what happened.

I am very honored that the Commission for the Just of Yad Vashem, after due deliberation, bestow upon me and my late wife Jeltje the Medal of the Just.

I accept your honor in great humiliation and thank you for your acknowledgement for what happened so long ago."

April 27, 1976

The medal was given to Jacob [Jaap] Simon Oversloot at Consulate General of Israel,[96] a high-rise office building in Los Angeles near Beverly Hills, on April 27, 1976. When I arrived at the suite, there was a very tiny outer office with one steel door and a buzzer. I gave my name, was allowed to go through the steel bombproof door, and was escorted to a very large luxurious office of antiques, wood floors and Asian carpets.

We had Dutch cookies and tea as refreshments. In attendance was Jacob S. Oversloot (Dad), Martha Van Buren-Oversloot (Dad's second wife), Julia Oversloot-Clauser (daughter), Jack Oversloot (son), H Warnaar (Consul General of The Netherlands), Malka Ben-Yosef, (Consul of Press and Information, Israel) and Hayin Hefer (Consul Cultural Affairs, Consulate General of Israel, Los Angeles).

Afterward, Dad took Martha, Jack and I to the best restaurant in town for lunch, "Scandia."

The Right thing to Do

At the time of the interview with Robert in 2010, I explained what Jacob said when he received the Yad Vashem award. Consul Warnaar of The Netherlands asked my dad, *"Why did you do this?"*

Jaap said, *"It was the right thing to do"* after a long pause he continued, *"If I am going to die, it is going to be for the right reason."*

Rob response, *"That is Christianity at its finest. Right? If you live life decently, if someone decides to kill you that is very awful. You are right; it is the killer who is wrong. There is your definition of good and evil. That is how these good people thought. There are people trying to work on it to tease out the ingredients. The only ingredient is simple – the only test question I would ask myself is 'What would I do under those circumstances?' I hope I am not put to the test because 'I don't know what I would do.'*"

---

96 At 6380 Wilshire Boulevard, Suite 1700, Los Angeles, CA 90048.

Aunt Jel and Uncle Jaap

Robert said, *"What was so endearing about your parents is they did not set out to be heroes. It is such a wrong concept. The heroism was just common human decency. If you're a good Christian, you save people. Your father could not understand why Christians were killing. How could you be a Christian and a killer? It was impossible. Can you imagine a Nazi catholic working all day at a concentration camp then going home after killing people all day and playing with his children? It would have been a concept incompatible with how your Dad lived his life."*

Displaced Persons

"Many Jewish survivors could not return home."
– Michael Berenbaum

Until I did research for this book, I had no idea what happened to all the people in the concentration camp or the armies. Freedom occurred for different people at different times as the allies moved to free that country or that camp. These people's struggles should not be forgotten.

"As the Allied armies swept through Europe in 1944 and 1945, they found seven to nine million displaced persons ["DP"] living in countries not their own. [Soldiers and people in hiding.] More than six million returned to their native lands. But more than one million refused repatriation. Most of them were Poles, Estonians, Latvians, Lithuanians, Ukrainians, and Yugoslavians. Some had collaborated with the Nazis and were afraid of retaliation if they returned home. Others feared persecution by the new Communist regimes in Eastern Europe ... .

"Many Jewish survivors could not return home. Their communities were shattered and their homes destroyed or occupied by strangers.

Dachau survivors gather by the moat to greet Americans, April 9, 1945, {#01100A. U.S. Holocaust Memorial Museum, courtesy of the National archives and Records Administration, College Park.}

In the east, they were not welcome in the land of their birth. With nowhere to go, Jewish displaced persons often had to live in camps set up on the sites where they had been imprisoned. For most of them, this meant a prolonged stay in Germany [and Poland] living in the midst of those who had sought to impose the 'Final Solution' on them … .

"The survivors were destitute and often sick. After liberation, the inhabitants of the DP camps were often dirty. If they were not depressed, they were argumentative. They were haunted by nightmares and mistrusted authority – even the American authorities who were trying to help them. Living in Germany [and Poland] in camps that also housed people who openly hated the Jews did little to improve their morale … ."[97]

Britain own Palestine – part of which became Israel

"Most Jewish displaced persons wanted to begin a new life in Palestine. Although many would have preferred to emigrate to the United States, but they were not willing to wait for years to qualify for admission … .

"Britain was unwilling to permit Jewish emigration to Palestine [or divide that country to allow for the State of Israel within its borders]. Trying to preserve the remnants of its empire, it was reluctant to alienate the Arab world hostile to a potential Jewish state. The United States was not ready to receive an influx of refugees. Soldiers were coming home from the war. It was a time of transition from war production to a civilian economy, and there was a fear that refugees would consume scarce resources and take jobs away from Americans … .

"Within weeks of taking office President, Harry Truman dispatched Earl Harrison, the Dean of University of Pennsylvania Law School, to report on the displaced person camps. The report was a bombshell… . His recommendations were sweeping; the special status of Jews must be recognized; they should be evacuated from Germany swiftly; and 100,000 Jews should be admitted to Palestine. Truman, who was later to become a hero to the Jews for recognizing Israel as a State, followed his humanitarian impulse.

---

97 Berenbaum, Michael, *The World Must Know*, Johns Hopkins University Press, 1993, pg 208.

He endorsed the report, rebuked the army, and intensified the pressure on Britain to allow 100,000 Jews to immigrate to Palestine … . His personal sentiments were clear: 'It is unthinkable that they should be left indefinitely in camps in Europe… .'

"Slowly, the survivors renewed their lives. At first, the DP camps consisted primarily of single men. Fewer women had survived. Life was lonely. Relief agencies such as the United Nations Relief and Rehabilitation Administration (UNRRA) took care of the basic daily needs, but in the fall of 1945, Jewish relief organizations came pouring into the camps. Personnel from the Jewish Agency and the Jewish Brigade worked with the survivors. They started schools and agricultural farms. They taught Hebrew and began the preliminary organizing that would make the displaced person a potent political force on behalf of the establishment of a Jewish state in Palestine."[98]

Immigration to America

"During the three years after the war, only 41,000 DPs were admitted to the United States. Two thirds of them were Jews. [Then] in the four years following the passage of the immigration laws of 1948 and 1950, 365,223 displaced persons were brought to American shores. Half the immigrants were Roman Catholic and only 16% Jews. Some of the DPs openly admitted to having collaborated with the Nazis. All in all, fewer than 100,000 Jews were able to reach the United States in the years between the end of the war and the expiration of the Displaced Person Act on December 31, 1952."[99]

The Hidden Children

The 'Hidden Children' were Jewish children born between 1927 to 1943 that were separated from their parents and family during the occupation. In Robert's 1993 lecture he discussed that, *"Some children were with hiders who abused them sexually, beat them, and exploited them as slave labor. Many children were moved a dozen times,*

---

98 *Ibid.*, pg 208.
99 *Ibid.*, pg 212.

Leo, Robert & Emmy c. 1941 {K}. Photo on the cover of the book.

often at night, to different homes and hiding places. Most lived in fear – of not being lovable, looking too Jewish, of being in the way,"[100]

Robert was one of the lucky ones. He was never in a DP camp. He was claimed by his mother and father though he did not like it very much the first couple of weeks and months. He was more comfortable with his foster parents, whom he called *Moeder* and *Vader*. Robert's parents had to persuade Robert he was theirs with photographs such as this one to the right.

Displaced Children

"Children under six accounted for 8.5% of the camps' Jewish population and 12% of the inmates were between the ages of 6-17. By that time also, nearly 1,000 babies were being born each month. There were no more than 26,000 children in the camps, 5,700 of them orphans."[101] Some of the surviving children were spirited away to England and some to France.

The doctors of the time did not think these hidden children could live productive normal lives. They were wrong. Robert writes, "A psychiatrist told a group of Jewish children at Ecouis [in France]; the 500 or so children gathered from Buchenwald, that they would never recover.

"We now know that this group has produced Elie Wiesel, Nobel Prize winning author and activist, the little boy Luleck, the youngest survivor of Buchenwald who is the Chief Rabbi of Israel, Rabbi Meier Lau, and his brother Nafthalie Lavie, who became Israel's Consul General to New York. Amongst that group also are physicians and physicists, artists and teachers, and those like you and me who have done our very best, quietly, in comparative silence or anonymity."[102]

---

100 Krell, Robert, *Child Holocaust Survivor*, Trafford Publishing, 2007, Lecture in 1993 pg 64.
101 Krell, Robert, *Child Holocaust Survivor*, Trafford Publishing, 2007, Lecture in 2000 pgs 125-126.
102 Krell, Robert, *Child Holocaust Survivor*, Trafford Publishing, 2007, Lecture in 1995 pg 85.

Rob continues, *"Once recovered from famine, and severe illness, children began their search for surviving family ... . It was difficult for children to rebuild an identity if they were too young to recall meaningful memories. Older children with recollections, however painful, were able to rebuild, from scraps and pieces, a sense of who they were ... . Those who did not recover family stayed in DP camps or drifted back to children's centers. For [those] children, the war lasted on average five to six more years after the day of liberation."[103]*

Survivors Married[104]

Many who had lost a spouse remarried. Rabbis were particularly lenient in their interpretation of Jewish law to permit remarriage. By tradition, a widow may not remarry unless eyewitnesses had seen her husband dead, such ordinary evidence of death was not possible after the Holocaust ... . A survivor couched his marriage proposal in words framed by tragedy:

"I am alone. I have no one. I have lost everything. You are alone. You
have no one. You have lost everything. Let us be alone together...
Life was renewed even as memories of death lingered."[105]

Second Generation
(Do not confuse them with the Hidden Children)

The children of these newly married survivors are called Second Generation Children. They were born after the war.

---

103 *Ibid.*, Lecture in 2000 pg 126.
104 Berenbaum, Michael, *The World Must Know,* Johns Hopkins University Press, 1993, pgs 209,210.
105 *Ibid,* pg 209.

Robert notes, *"The mystery is how in fact the second generation offspring of these adult survivors became disproportionately represented in the helping professions. This issue is somewhat clearer in the children of child survivors who themselves are frequently working in professions concerning children or the aged or conducting research into topics concerning the human condition.*

"The survivor parents attempted to protect their children from knowing of their horrible experiences which ran counter to the child's need to know. The 'silence' on this topic was filled by childhood fantasies occasionally even more horrifying than knowing. Protecting the child sometimes exacerbated and complicated more ordinary family problems."[106]

---

106 Krell, Robert, *Child Holocaust Survivor*, Trafford Publishing, 2007, Lecture in 2004 pg 155.

Conclusion

Historian Yehuba Bauer enunciated three commandments
as the human imperative to the Holocaust:
"Thou shalt not be a victim.
Thou shalt not be a perpetrator.
Above all, thou shalt not be a bystander."[107]

– Yehuba Bauer

These commandments apply to everyone – everywhere – now and always.

By acts of defiance, both couples survived. My parents helped to save a Jewish couple because they were decent caring people. Others did the same—some survived and some did not. It was a matter of luck and being smart about how much you told other people. Leo became an Uncle, Emmy an Aunt and daily life went on. The Occupation put burdens and fears in everyone's life. There were traitors all around us. Taking a day at a time was the best they could do. Worrying about more than yourself and your family was unusual.

They were lucky to meet, that Dad became friends with Leo and then Emmy and that they cared about the infant Robert. That there was money to be made as furriers. Where did they find the pelts? Who did they pay to make the lining for the coats? Where did they get food every day? How many other people did they kept alive by providing them an income? They were lucky to have enough food to eat until almost the end of the war.

There are many questions but the main thing is that they survived. The extended Krell and Stelzer families and most of their friends were not so fortunate. They were worked to death, starved, died from illness, or murdered. Living with survivor's guilt was painful. Memories would always creep back while rebuilding their lives. Post-war was a time when no one wanted to hear the stories of survival.

---

107 Berenbaum, Michael, *The World Must Know,* Johns Hopkins University Press, 1993, pg 224.

However, the Krells did the extra step of listening and trying to put families back together after the war.

It is painful for us to remember the facts that allowed the Holocaust to happen. It was painful that so many facts were unknown until after the war. We need to remember and try our best to fight racism and prejudice within ourselves and stand up for those less fortunate to stop this cycle.

What have I learned from writing this book?
- That human beings' will to survive is very strong. That when rights are removed the level of survival decreases. However, people do what they must to survive. The ability to do anything against the Nazi was slim.
- That blood is thicker than water and people would rather die as a family together than survive alone unless absolutely necessary. The need for parents to keep their children safe is of utmost importance.
- That every family member's death is devastating but in the end, you must live for the moment to survive. Many worked hard to survive just to tell the stories that it will "Never Happen Again."
- That absolute power corrupts absolutely. That "good" does not win over "evil" but there is some good everywhere that some survival is possible.
- It is human to forget the horrible in order to continue life, but we need to remember to talk about the events to prevent history from recurring and for good mental health.

Discussion Questions

1. Do you have a grandparent that is a Jew?
   • Would it be fair for you to be classified as a Jew and be put to death?
2. Could you have been strong enough to survive?
3. Could you have helped another person?
4. Would you have maintained thoughts of decency to others:
   • Even under the stress of war and occupation?
   • Even if you were starving?
   • Even if someone threatened your life or the life of a love one?
   • Even if you were numb from being worked to death?
5. If you were lucky enough to survive, could you have continued a normal life?

My Hope

It is my hope that you've learned something from reading the story of the Oversloots and the Krells, as I have. We can apply this knowledge by helping others, reduce racism, and prejudice.

It is within your power!

If you would like to ensure "Decency" continues, share the stories in the book and be an example of Decency.

How you can help to spread Decency

If you would like to do more, please consider a contribution to one of the following. They each are great organizations for educating the public against racism and prejudice.

United States Holocaust Museum (http://www.ushmm.org/)
100 Raoul Wallenberg Place SW
Washington, D.C. 20024-2126

Righteous Among the Nations Department – Yad Vashem
(http://www.yadvashem.org/yv/en/righteous/)
Martyrs' and Heroes' Remembrance Authority
P O B 3477
Jerusalem, 9103401 Israel
Email: Righteous Among the Nations (righteous.nations@yadvashem.org.il)

Vancouver Holocaust Educational Centre (VHEC)[108]
(http://www.vhec.org/)
50 – 950 West 41st Avenue
Vancouver, BC V5Z 2N7
Email: VHEC (Info@VHEC.org)

---

108 The Vancouver Holocaust Centre Society was founded in 1983 by **Dr. Robert Krell**, hidden child survivor of the Holocaust. His goal for the foundation was realized in 1994. It was to leave a permanent legacy in the form of the Vancouver Holocaust Education Centre ("VHEC") devoted to Holocaust based anti-racism education.

The Vancouver Holocaust Education Centre is a teaching museum and a leader in Holocaust education in British Columbia, reaching over 25,000 students annually. It produces acclaimed exhibits, innovative school programs and teaching materials, including online exhibits. The VHEC presents numerous public cultural and commemorative events. It publishes a quarterly newsletter and Holocaust-related books. The VHEC maintains a museum collection and archives, a survivor testimony project, as well as a library and resource centre.

APPENDICES

Testimonial by Robert Krell[109]

This is my testimony of survival in acknowledgement to the Dutch family who protected me in the war years 1942-1945.

Robert Krell c. 1980's {K}

March 30, 1975
… Occupation: Psychiatrist
Place of residence during war: Loenenschestraat 147, Den Haag, Holland

Rescuers
Mr. Albertus Hendrik Munnik – deceased 1972
Mrs. Violette Munnik – Hendriks
Den Haag, Holland
Mrs. Nora Munnik – Lorier
Niewesluistraat 201
Den Haag, Holland

To Ms. Donia Rosen
Head, Department for the Righteous Yad Vashem Memorial

    I shall tell you briefly my story in the hope that the Munnik family shall be inscribed as Righteous Gentiles.
    I was born in The Hague, Holland. My parents are Eliasz and Estera Krell. We lived in a house on the Suezkade. Holland was occupied and the Germans were already imposing restrictions on Jews. We received notice in 1942 to board trains for 're-settlement' on August 19th of that year. The destination of these trains was Auschwitz.

---

109 I obtained a copy of letter from Robert Krell 2010. The original is at the *Yad Vashem* museum. This is the complete letter without editing. I added meaningful photos that were obtained from Robert.

Most of my parents' friends went and never returned. My parents through foresight and with courage decided that we should go into hiding. My mother approached a friend to take me for a few days while she found a place to hide.

On that day, a Mrs. Munnik by chance dropped in to visit this lady. She offered to take me for several weeks and ended up sheltering me for 3 ½ years. To her, this chance meeting remains to this day a 'Miracle' in her eyes. Mr. Munnik became as of that day, my father and Nora (age 10) my sister. He treated me as his son until his death.

There is little need to explain that the Munnik family risked death in suddenly acquiring a 2 ½ year old dark-haired son. I was taught to call my real parents 'aunt' and 'uncle' as a child would with close friends who are not relatives. My parents visited from time to time and my father provided all of us with food.

My own recall goes back to age 2 ½ or thereabouts. I sat on my father's lap and warned him (as my uncle) to be careful. I could feel the gun he carried as I pressed against him.

We ate tulip bulbs and my Moeder would tell us they were potatoes because she was ashamed to tell us there were none. My Vader on occasion brought home a rabbit to eat—he killed it with his bicycle pump and the carcass hung in the kitchen. Outside, German soldiers marched around the square. From our front window, we could see them and sometimes V2 rockets were fired over The Hague. One looked to fall close by but it was only an illusion.

Life was pleasant for me. I suffered little. For the most part, I stayed inside. Nora was pleasant and patient and taught me to read when I was four. The Munniks were loving people possessed of a deep, but not necessarily religious faith. They never imposed on me beliefs, which could interfere with the acquisition of Judaism and its traditions.

V - E Day I remember well. Crowds celebrated in the streets and British planes dropped food parcels. White bread was considered the greatest treat.

The most traumatic event of all was returning to my own Mom and Dad. They had to prove to me through pictures that I was theirs. I went with them, reluctant and tearful. I cried not so much for going with my real parents but for having to leave my Moeder, Vader and Nora.

I was now about 5 ½ and we lived at the Spuistraat 149. Our living room became a sort of reception centre for the remnants of The Hague Jewry. Each day I saw people in such despair and heard stories so frightening that I have never forgotten them. I listened pretending not to understand either the language or the content. The adults spoke in front of us children because they thought their words and experiences were not understood.

I suppose what is unique about my story is that my parents survived and remained close and faithful friends with my rescuers. In fact, they shared me. I saw the Munnik's frequently. They visited and often travelled with my parents. I stayed with them when my parents went on trips alone.

My father's parents and his two sisters perished. All but one of my two aunts' children died. The surviving first cousin remained with his Dutch foster parents.

My mother's parents, 2 brothers and one sister perished. Few friends were left in Holland after the war. It was not the place to begin life anew. In 1950,[110] we immigrated to Canada. It was a good decision although I missed my Moeder and Vader terribly for some time. In 1961, at age 20, I visited with them in Holland. My room was intact and waiting for me, furnished as it had been in 1945. On the wall is a testimonial to their having sheltered me.

In 1965 I graduated in Medicine from the University of British Columbia at Vancouver. My parents arranged for Moeder and Vader to be present. It was their first trip to a foreign land.

In 1971 I married in Vancouver. It was a unique event. My wife's parent and my two sets of parents were all there. My brother Ron (born in Canada in 1956) was best man. Moeder delivered a spontaneous speech to the 400 guests and I translated. Most guests were Jewish and many were themselves survivors. It was a happy, yet tearful event.

---

110 The Krells emigrated left Rotterdam to Canada on 24 March 1951 arriving in Seattle 20 April 1951 not 1950 on the Holland-American Line ship called the *"Diemerdyk."* Evidence obtained from Ancestry.com shipping documents.

Vader was already ill at that time. He had difficulty swallowing and had a choking cough. He was briefly hospitalized in Vancouver and then returned to Holland. Vader died several months later.

He worked for the city water department all his life. His humility and simplicity belied his intelligence, his quick wit and his many talents. Wherever he went, people were irresistibly drawn to him. His humor and sparkling eyes required no translation—everyone could understand him. No one who has met him has ever forgotten him. He was a just man. To me he seemed saintly: an earthy, jovial saint who was totally open and not subject to fierce inner struggles. He did what had to be done.

My Moeder inspired him and supported him. They complemented each other. I saw her again the summer of 1974. She missed him desperately as he would have her, had she passed away. And yet Moeder is not depressed for even now the strength of their relationship sustains her.

These remarkable people felt that the war, as tragic as it was, brought them a son which is how God had meant it to be. My staying with them was viewed as an act of God and that was that. The issues of fear or danger or sacrifice simply did not exist for them.

My Moeder hoped I would be a doctor who would help children. In fact, she felt that I had been saved for that purpose. I am probably the only Jewish child psychiatrist prodded by his Christian rather than his Jewish parents.

Honor this family. We will need more like them for it is not yet over.

Yours respectfully,
Robert Krell

[Note on Robert's letter to Ms. Donia Rosen dated August 27, 1975 was that "Mr. Moshe Yuval, Political Advisor, was the most gracious person and empathic interviewer."]

Robert Krell's Biography

Brief Biography provided by Robert Krell – M.D. F.R.C.P. (C), July 2011

Professor Emeritus
Department of Psychiatry
The University of British Columbia

Dr. Krell was born in The Hague, Holland on August 5th 1940. He was hidden from 1942 to 1945 with the Munnik family and returned to his parents who also survived in hiding. Their families of origin were all murdered in Auschwitz and Sobibor.

In 1951, the Krell's moved to Vancouver, B.C. Robert Krell graduated from The University of British Columbia with an M.D. in 1965, interned in Philadelphia at the Philadelphia General Hospital, and continued in psychiatric training at Temple University Hospital, Philadelphia, Stanford University Hospital in Palo Alto and then returned to The University of British Columbia.

In 1970 he became an F.R.C.P.(C) and in 1971 a Diplomat of the American Boards of Psychiatry and Neurology. A UBC Assistant Professor in Psychiatry he served as Professor of Psychiatry until 1995, when he became Professor Emeritus. He was Director of Residency Training for ten years and for twenty-five years the Director of Child and Family Psychiatry at the UBC Health Sciences Centre.

As a volunteer in the community, Robert Krell served on the Board of Directors of the Canadian Jewish Congress-Pacific Region from 1972, was Vice Chair for nine years, Chair from 1986-1989 and National Vice President from 1989-1992.

During that time he initiated in 1975, with Dr. Graham Forst of Capilano College as co-Chair, the Standing Committee on Holocaust Education, which teaches more than 1,000 British Columbia high school students annually. Outreach programs serve additional thousands of students in the Interior and on Vancouver Island. The program serves as an educational tool to combat prejudice and racism.

In his private psychiatric practice, Dr. Krell treated Holocaust survivors and their families and Dutch survivors of Japanese concentration camps.

Dr. Krell began audiovisual documentation in the Vancouver area in 1978 and expanded this program in 1983 and 1984 to tape 120 eyewitness accounts. In 1980 he urged the Canadian Jewish Congress to establish a national program, which resulted in a nationwide audiovisual project taping 70 survivors.

Being himself a child survivor of the Holocaust, he assisted with the formation of child survivor groups, first in Los Angeles between 1983 and 1984 and then in Vancouver more recently. He served on the International Advisory Council of the Hidden Child Conference that organized a gathering in New York in 1991 for approximately 1,500 child survivors who came from many countries to meet for the first time.

In 1985 Dr. Krell founded the Vancouver Holocaust Centre Society for Education and Remembrance which built a memorial for Holocaust survivors, unveiled in 1987 at the Schara Tzedeck Cemetery.

Dr. Krell established a Holocaust Education Centre, which opened on November 7th 1994 in order to continue teaching programs for high school children as a warning of the consequences of unchecked racism and intolerance. For these activities he received in 1998 the State of Israel Bonds Elie Wiesel Remembrance Award.

He has co-edited and authored six books, many book chapters and journal articles. Recent books include:

"The Children of Buchenwald and Their Postwar Lives" by Judith Hemmendinger and Robert Krell. Jerusalem: Gefen Publishing. 2000.

"And Life is Changed Forever: Holocaust Childhoods Remembered" edited by Norman Glassner and Robert Krell. Detroit: Wayne State University Press. 2006.

"Child Holocaust Survivors: Memories and Reflections" by Robert Krell with contributions by Haim Dasberg, Martin Gilbert, Sarah Moskovitz and Elie Wiesel, Trafford Publishing, 2007.

Robert Krell has three children and six grand-children.

Tribute to Robert Krell

Elie Wiesel, survivor from Buchenwald, who was one of the first to write about his experience during the Holocaust and camps, received the Nobel Prize. He said this about Robert:

"Dr Krell established a Holocaust Education Centre, which opened on November 7th 1994 in order to continue teaching programs for high school children as a warning of the consequences of unchecked racism and intolerance. For these activities, he received in 1998 the 'State of Israel Bonds Elie Wiesel Remembrance Award.'

"Robert and I have become so close because of what he felt he had to tell and to give to so many of his students, patients and friends and I feel the same about my students and my friends and all the children who are linked to mine. I feel moved in your presence. I look at you and I must tell you the truth. I look at you and I remember other children. Other Jewish children who could not find hiding places. Death alone wanted their company. I think of them at times with anger as much as with sorrow. How many Nobel Laureates were there among them? Some of them might have developed cures for cancer, heart diseases, or AIDS.

"Others might have written poems and composed music of such force that they would have sensitized multitudes to the evil of indifference and war. In allowing a million and more Jewish children to die, humankind inflicted suffering and punishment on itself as well. But then I look at you again and feel rewarded. You have done something with your orphaned memories, something of which you could and should be proud. You have kept your childhood intact and you have built on it a temple for future children and parents to worship in and live in for the sake of one another. There is something about your hidden memories that makes me hesitate to touch them. Your hidden childhood suggests intense pain, profound darkness and an infinite need for tenderness, gentleness and human warmth.

Elie Wiesel c. 1991 {RK}.

Yet that thirst for tenderness and love is also what makes you smile and dream. It is what makes me smile and dream. So after these days of encounters, I suggest that from now on you think of your hidden childhood, not only with fear or sadness, but think of it also with joy and hope and gratitude." [111]

---

111 Krell, Robert, *Child Holocaust Survivors*, Trafford Publishing, Canada, 2007, Chp 5, *Hidden Memories*, by Elie Wiesel 1991, pgs 50-51.

Testimonial by Leo Krell [112]

Robert submitted the request for the medal to be given to the Munniks and Oversloots in 1975. He did not know all the details for the Oversloots so asked his dad to write a letter to *Yad Vashem*. The letter is as follows:

April 6, 1975
Rescued:
Robert Krell
Parents:
Eliasz Krell (Leo Krell)
B.D. Sept. 3, 1913
Vancouver, B.C. Canada

Leo Krell c. 1947 {K}

Manager: Real Estate Apartment Sales
Estera (Emmy) Krell
B.D. June 2, 1915
Vancouver, B.C. Canada
Residence during the war: The Hague, Holland

Robert, we called him Robbie, was born August 5, 1940. On the previous 10th of May, the Germans had attacked and the battle for survival started. Every day, new laws were made mainly to make life for Jews miserable. In about the middle of 1941, the Judenrat was established; its job to register all Jews to make sure, as we found out later, nobody was to survive. We had some good Gentile friends and by discussing with them the circumstances, we decided to fight, not to give in to any of the German Regulations.

Leo Krell c. 1991

---

112 This is a complete body of the letter written by Leo Krell that has not been edited. It was either obtained from Robert Krell and/or Righteous Among the Nations Department of *Yad Vashem* in Israel.

By June 1942, we knew already several people who were picked up by the enemy and did not return. At the same time, I had to appear first before the 'Judenrat' in Amsterdam, then for later visits to the Gestapo headquarters in the same place. They commanded me to return in a few days and deliver to them a list of my clients (I was a furrier), list all furs in my possession, bring my insurance papers, passport, documents and proof of all our possessions. I had to fill out an application for Rob, Em and myself for what they called "Vrijwillige Emigratie" [Voluntary Emigration] *which I refused to do. Again, I got a few days respite. Rob was at that time not quite 2 years old.*

We lived in fear a few more months. With a family who were our friends, we decided to use part of their attic and prepare it so that I could stay there without coming down too much. That family's name was Jacob S Oversloot, his wife Jeltje, and there were four little children. Em was supposed to stay where Robbie went, but things were to be different than planned. In this most strenuous time, we had another Gentile couple who visited our place practically every day to lend moral support and to help us if the need should arise. Her name was Mrs. Mulder and his name was Hol. 'Opa Hol' we called him. This was during the time no Gentile was supposed to visit or collaborate with a Jew.

From here on we were harassed, the telephones taken out, bicycles and public transportation prohibited, regulation to wear a yellow star, shopping only after 5 pm when all was sold out etc – the old Jewish story.

In the evening of August 18, 1942, when curfew was 8 pm [no-one allowed outside after 8], some men came to the front door to deliver three letters, stating that we had to be the 19th of August at 1am [really the beginning of the 20th] at the railway station for the first part of our last trip, to Camp 'Westerbork.' The letter stated to take not too much and nothing heavy, but to take blankets, some clothing - I guess to make it look real. The actual idea was to get you to close the door behind you and leave everything so the Gestapo could pick it all up and give it to the German people.

*Our departure from home was planned for after 8 pm [remember the curfew].
This was done by the Gestapo to undermine chances of avoiding the rules. Now
the action started. We packed, mainly light stuff but looking heavy. We put Rob in
a buggy and left, with the neighbors watching. We left around 6 [PM] taking for
granted that people would not know the precise time of arrangement in our letters.*

*We had a 10-minute walk to the house of Opa Hol and Mrs. Mulder. According-
ing to plan, Em and Robbie stayed there. I was supposed to go to J Oversloot. All
went well for a few days when Mrs. Oversloot got sick and had to go to the hospital
leaving her husband, four kids and me at home. We asked Em for help and she did.
She left Rob for a few days with the Mulders and joined the Oversloot household.
Em looked after the four kids, the men, the cleaning, everything-but had not chance
to see Rob. The German roundup of Jews, the curfew, and all the troubles together
took a few weeks. Our contact with Rob was through Jaap Oversloot. He came home
telling us he is well, looks good and doesn't cry.*

*But now the big news came. Opa Hol and Mrs. Mulder were called in by the
German decree, which wanted all older people out of the city. They were willing
to take the child but we protested. We did not want to take our chances outside
The Hague.*

*We then got a message that Mulder and Hol had friends who Hol used to work
with. They would take Rob, no questions asked, knowing we were Jewish. We met
those wonderful people and they were the three Munniks. First, they told us not to
worry. If they ate, Rob too would eat and that while bringing up their daughter,
they would temporarily bring up a son, until times got better. Then they would give
him back.*

*Now Rob was over 2 years of age, called them Vader and Moeder, which is
Dutch for parents. We became uncle and aunty and the family was informed that
they had a child of Jewish parents who had to go to camp. We had to stay clear. Arrangements were made so we could visit once a week and had to walk more than one
hour each way and watch and hope that all was well during the past week.*

Financially what the Munniks did could not be paid for at that time. Let us say that what we paid and what we gave them was only enough to get through the worst time. In this time, we looked for another place for ourselves, mainly to take the pressure off. We decided to split the Krell family three ways and Rob stayed where he was. What a risk those people took.

After a few months, there were no Jews in The Hague. Sure, the Germans missed some but not many. New laws were made. Anyone who helps, hides, or collaborates with a Jew and does not turn him or her in, will be shot if and when caught. We told the Munniks this. Their reply was 'we are not religious but if God wills it that all of us survive then we will and you will get back your son.' Mrs. Munnik added in one of our conversations that maybe the Lord wants him to live and be a doctor; he is such a good child.

In total, Rob must have spent approximately 4 weeks in Opa Hol's home which brings us to the end of September, 1942. He then stayed with the Munniks until the middle of May 1945. We missed him roughly from age 2 to 5. We saw him almost weekly and our coming to visit never was a burden to them. Mr. Munnik died in late 1973. We lost a good friend, Rob lost a father. Today, 1975, Robert is a doctor.

This is a compact true story. Any required details will be supplied on request.

Leo Krell and Emmy Krell

Letter to Granddaughters by Emmy Krell

I received a copy of the "Letter to Granddaughters" by Emmy Krell on February 6, 2012 from Robert Krell. It revealed many facts that I was not aware of and balanced the information in this book.

Vancouver
October 22, 1985

Emmy Krell in 1991.

    I think you will be interested in your Daddy's (Marnie's Uncle Robs) of the first five-years when he was growing up in Holland during the war.

    Before the war, we were all very happy living in a kind of fairytale, beautiful country, with a Queen who was called Wilhelmina and her daughter, Princess Juliana. Holland was a country of hard working people, involved with their families, loving their children, having respect for all kinds of religion and education. The government was supportive towards all kinds of churches, synagogues and schools. People had free choice to go to all of them or to any one of them.

    On 1st of September 1939, without any warning, the Germans started a war with Poland. Germany had been preparing for years to start the thousand-year Reich – their plan to rule the world. Hating the Polish people as they did, Germany invaded Poland and with their superior weapons, they were able to occupy the defenseless country within two weeks. Then the Germans turned against France, Belgium and Holland.

    One day, our Prime Minister, Dr. Dress,[113] talked to the Dutch people on the radio. His speech went like this, 'People of Holland, we have nothing to worry about; we are going to stay neutral; we are not going to war with anyone; we have no weapons to fight a war with, and to my knowledge we own only three planes.

---

113 Emmy letter indicates Dr Willem Drees was the Prime Minister, however he did not get into office until 1948, 1951-1952. The Prime Minister during this period was Dirk Jan deGeer. {Wiki}.

But we took steps to have plenty of food for our people to last about six years and these supplies are stored mostly in coolers in the Port of Rotterdam.' Unfortunately, being an honest man, Mr. Dress had also revealed to the Germans where the food was stored. Mr. Dress finished his speech to the Dutch people with encouraging words to the effect that, 'We have very brave soldiers and the people to back them up to defend our beloved country'

Oma has a saying, "Some bad things happen overnight."

On 10 May 1940, Holland was attacked by the Germans. Aeroplanes, called 'Stukas', which looked like big black bats, bombed the cities. Parachuters from some of the planes dropped out of the skies disguised as Nuns, Priests, civilians, and hidden in their clothing were weapons to attack anyone who was in their way. The Dutch soldiers who were near the border between Germany and Holland tried to fight back. The Germans said, 'We are going to bomb Rotterdam and flatten it to the ground' and half of Rotterdam was burned and destroyed, and thirty thousand people were killed. The Dutch soldiers were still trying to hold back the German invaders and so the Germans told the Dutch people to stop fighting or they would do that to other cities what they had done to Rotterdam.

It was like living through a nightmare; like a scene from a Spielberg movie— or even worse because it was really happening it was the real thing. That night, Queen Wilhelmina, Princess Juliana and Prince Bernard left Holland and went to England.

The next morning on the radio, we listened to the announcer. His words were, "Listen to the voices that are known to you. We are the Dutch people"—and silence. He was shot and the Germans took over the radio station and told us that we had no Government anymore and we were now all prisoners of war and everything would be alright if we just followed their regulations—but we did not know what their regulation would be or how harsh they would be. We were soon to learn.

We were not allowed to have a radio or a telephone; we had to give our bikes to the Germans; everything that was gold, silver or copper had to be given over to them—everything that was valuable was taken away from us. The Germans went after our lives. In the middle of the night they would pick up all the highly educated people first, they disappeared and nobody heard from them again. For the Jews they had even stricter regulation. They had to wear on their coats the Star of David, which made them visible, if they went into streets, which were restricted to them. They were arrested by the Germans and put into concentration camps.

Now girls, to continue with the story from the time your Daddy decided to be born, August 5th, in the middle of a big air raid, and on the same day, that Princess Irene was born.[114] When I arrived at the hospital, the nurses who, like most Dutch people, loved our Royal Family told me that if the baby was a girl I must call her Irene. As you know, your Daddy was a boy and I could hardly have called him Irene! So he was named Robert.

In every ward in the hospital there was a least ten hungry mothers as the other wards were full of wounded German Soldiers. We got very little to eat as the food supplies were given to the solders. We were afraid of the nights as that was when the city was attacked from the air. Yes, we were hungry and frightened but we had our babies and our husbands filled our rooms with flowers to let the Germans see that we were not losing hope. We were not much to the Germans but we meant a lot to each other. We were loyal to our country and helped each other every way we could. Sometimes sharing food, even though we had so little to share. We knew that we had to survive but our future did not seem very secure.

On 19th August 1942, when your Daddy was two years old, it was our turn to go to a camp with 6,000 other people including parents and children but we met some nice people during the summer who were willing to help us but they could only take the parents as they already had four children of their own and so another family took your Daddy.

---

114 Irene was born August 5, 1939—same day but the previous year.

To be separated from your child is a very hard thing but we wanted badly to save his life and this was the only thing we could do. We prayed the separation from our son would only be for a short time because there was talk of a Blitz Krieg—a short war. We never thought about losing the war even with the Germans occupying our cities and treating us very harshly. We had something higher to believe in than just Hitler—we had our religion and we were not killers—we believed in the commandments—'Thou Shalt Not Kill'—because killing is not the solution to anything.

Your Daddy lived six-weeks with a lady called J.M. who had also a little boy of 11years and old and a gentleman who was called Opa. He [Robert] did not like it very much to be away from his parents and later he left this family and went to live with another family, Mr. and Mrs. A. Munnik, who had a little girl of 10 years old and her name was Nora. They shared a room and we were very lucky that the little girl was not jealous of the little boy and she accepted him and loved him more than if he had been her little brother. She taught him to read and played with him and taught him to do all kinds of things.

It was a difficult task to keep the little boy a secret from the neighbors for he wanted to go out to play and if it were found out that the little boy should have not been living with this family it would have meant a lot of trouble for them and they were very brave people as their lives were at stake and the Germans would have dealt harshly with them.

Some neighbors knew the boy from before but we were lucky that they were on our side and they did not belong to the Nazi party and so the boy was safe and the people who had taken him in were safe. Finally, he came to believe that the people he stayed with were his parents and his real parents were known to him as his Aunt and Uncle.

The war went on for another three years. Most of the Jewish people ended up in concentration camps and only one per cent came back alive. Our family were all killed but we survived by hiding and being helped by our friends.

After the war, it was very hard for us to live in Holland without our family and friends who had all perished and so we decided to work very hard to get some money together. Then we sought a better life and decided to immigrate, first of all to America but it was easier to stay in Canada. Your Daddy was then over ten years of age when we came to Vancouver.

After a beautiful six-week trip on the boat thru the Panama Canal, we arrived in Vancouver. Soon we had a house and your Daddy started in school. The Principal of the school wanted to put your Daddy in first grade because he did not speak any English but I persuaded him to put him in Grade 4—the same grade that he was in Holland.

Because he was a good student, your Daddy soon learned to speak English— with the help of Connie's fist!!! Connie was the same age as your Daddy and one day I saw Connie holding up a fist to your Daddy and saying to him –'that's a tree and you had better remember that.' Connie was his main teacher in English.

There was no problem with your Daddy going to school because he was anxious to learn and he was liked by both his teachers and the other students. It was a difficult transition for us to settle in a new country where we did not speak the language but Rob understood and he cooperated and helped us in every way he could.

Our lives over here in Canada followed a pattern of most other immigrants in a new country. We made a good choice in picking Vancouver as our new home as it is the most beautiful city and we were happy.

I often wonder how much nicer life would have been if my little sister and Anne Frank had been alive and what contribution they would have brought to us. They were about the same age when they died from hunger. Reicele, my sister, not being three years old started on a second language and Anne Frank must have been very bright to leave behind her valuable thoughts on life and humanity.

Now, God gave me four little girls and I consider that a good sign to fill the empty places in my life. Not everyone was so lucky. And I say from my heart— thanks to God and let them and all children grow up in peace—along with Fluffy, the cat.

Love Ooma

"So We Don't Forget" Newspaper Article

"So We Don't Forget" — April 7, 1983

Altadenan Hid Jews From Nazi Occupiers[115]

By Arthur Wood

Now that the interview was over, Jacob Oversloot looked at the reporter for a long moment, his eyes thoughtful. During the conversation at his Altadena house he'd talked sometimes at length; at other moments he had been retiring, offering clippings from old newspapers to tell part of his story whenever his own words failed him.

In a telephone conversation two days before he had maintained, "I don't have a story." Now the quiet, modest man's reason for talking about himself at all became clear.

"I have only one request," he said. "You put on top of that story, 'So we don't forget'."

In a time when World War II and the Nazi extermination of the Jews was too long ago to be even a dim childhood memory for more than half the world's population, born after 1945, such a request seems like a tall order.

Oversloot is among those singled out by the Jewish Federation Council as the "Righteous Christians of the Holocaust," people who have been documented as helping Jews in German-occupied countries. Their simple decency led them to aid Jews by hiding them, helping them escape to safety and fighting the Germans along side Jews.

Oversloot has been honored before; a medal from the state of Israel lies in a safe deposit box. Next Sunday at the Scottish Rite Auditorium he will be honored again,

Jacob Oversloot, 1983
{Photo by Gary Mc Carthy}

---

115 Wood, Arthur, <u>Altadena/Pasadena. Chronicle</u>, April 7, 1983, "*So We Don't Forget*" pgs 1, 2 & 8. Copy retained by Jacob Oversloot.

at a program he would not attend, he says, were not the man whose parents he hid from the Nazis making a special trip to attend with him.

In May, 1940 the armored divisions of Germany poured out of the forest of the Argonne into France as parachute and mechanized troops rolled over the Low Countries, crushing the armies of Holland and Belgium.

In the Hague alone, 25,000 Jews were caught in a net of steel and bullets, along with Holland's other citizens. Jacob Oversloot and his wife, Jeltje, were among the Dutch Christians in that net.

At first, the Germans seemed to prefer securing voluntary cooperation from the occupied Dutch. With no real plan worked out yet for exterminating Jews, the Nazis began with requiring them to wear the Star of David on their clothing, as they had done in Germany.

Altadenan Saved Family

In 1942, Oversloot recalled, the deportations began. To man their factories and produce the weapons of war and consumer goods for the German people, the Nazis began taking the men, women and children of conquered countries to work as slave labor. "That was their excuse," he said.

By that time, they had also decided to exterminate every Jew they could find.

That was when a Jewish couple named Krell and their little boy came to Oversloot, asking for help, beginning a three-year odyssey of secrecy and fear, and a friendship that would last the rest of their lives.

The family, slated for Auschwitz, survived. The boy, taken in by a nearby family, the Munniks, became a professor at the University of British Columbia in Vancouver.

Oversloot, who eats a late and long lunch and never goes outside without some form of headgear, recalled how the unpleasant task of dividing the family came about.

Caption under the drawing of the house reads "Wartime Refuge – Oversloot home in The Hague served as a furrier's shop and home for Jewish friends during the Nazi Occupation."

"We couldn't take the little boy," he said, "because he was black [haired] and he wouldn't look like one of our children." Once the Star of David came off the clothing, the need to be inconspicuous centered around blending with the harboring families.

Oversloot, who was "not even 40 at the time," still had a thick shade of black in his now silvered hair. The two men decided they looked enough like relatives to fool the Germans, even though Leo Krell was shorter.

The occupation the two men shared made one a candidate for the ovens and the other unwanted for work in Germany.

"I was a furrier and he was a furrier," Oversloot observed. "I was in an occupation that they [the Germans] did not want." By becoming a "Dutch" furrier instead of a Jewish one Leo Krell achieved the same status.

The two couples lived in the Oversloot home where he and Krell conducted the fur business in Oversloot's attic. Their income was enough to by food, both the rationed variety and what was available on the black market.

During most of the nearly three years the Krells and Oversloots lived together, they were able to dine out occasionally as well as go about in town.

"We went out together," Oversloot said, adding that suspicion never seemed to fall on them. "If it had been the right sequence," he observed, "someone might have become suspicious, but no one did."

He never knew of anyone who was caught. "You knew someone was missing," he said, "but you never knew for sure."

The need for secrecy was such that even family members never were let in on what was happening.

When Oversloot's relatives would visit, "I told them it's family from wife's side," he said with a smile. When someone from my wife's side asked, I'd tell them he was from my side of the family."

The Krells eventually moved to an apartment of their own after the war to be with their son. After the war also, the two men opened a furrier's shop together.

By that time, the Krells were part of only 1,100 Jews remaining in the Hague.

"The Gestapo in the Hague was everywhere." Emmy Krell recalled in an interview some years ago at the age of 66. "Close calls? Plenty."

For Oversloot, though, the main fear came from the V-rockets that flew over Holland on their way to England.

He was afraid, he said, "not because of what we did, but because of the V-rockets they [the Germans] fired."

On the way to England, he said, the missiles developed by Werner Von Braun separated into several stages, "but sometimes they didn't make it," he recalled, and the different pieces, explosives and all, would plummet to the ground.

"You lie awake at night," he remembered as if suddenly transported back to his home in Holland, "Wondering if one would come down where you are."

But as for the rest of it," he said, "You've all got to die, you know.

"People asked me why I was hiding them in my house," he mused. "I said, 'Well, it's very simple. Hitler is ruling Europe. If I have to die in this war, I want to die for my own principles'."

"There were frequent dangers, but with a bunch of luck and a bunch of courage, we're alive today."

Glossary¹¹⁶

atelier — Workroom

c. — Circa approximate year

D Day — Invasion of Normandy, France on June 6, 1944 by the allied forces. U.S. Army troops wade ashore on Omaha Beach during the landings at 6:30 am.

Den Haag — In English, The Hague and/or *s-Gravenhage* in Dutch

Final Solution — Heinrich Himmler was the chief architect of Germany's plan and execution of the systematic genocide of European Jews during WWII.

Gentile — Non-Jew; someone who believes in Jesus.

Gestapo — **Ge**beim **Sta**atspo**l**izer=Secret State Police of Nazi Germany under SS leader Heinrich Himmler.

Guilder — A unit of Dutch currency that in 1940 was equivalent to 53 U.S. cents.

Judenrat — The headquarters where Jews were to report in Amsterdam.

Mein Kampf — Hitler's book "My Struggle" published in 1922.

Moeder — Dutch for Mother

N.S.B. — Nationaal-Socialistische Beweging Der Nederlanden (N.S.B.). National Socialist Movement of The Netherlands. The Dutch Nazi party headed by A. A. Mussert.

Oma — Grandmother in Dutch

Oom — Uncle in Dutch

Opa — Grandfather in Dutch

Peperzak — The name of the Fur Store Leo and Jacob owned in The Hague

SS — *Schutzstaffel*. Security Squad. The security organization of the German Nazi party, which became the heart of the Nazi totalitarian state under Himmler. The Dutch S.S. copied the initials of the Germans organization although the letters S.S. had no meaning in Dutch. Also, know as Paramilitary organization of which Allegmeine SS, Waffen SS, and Germanische SS. They wore black uniforms.

---

116 Sources are from reading materials, Wikipedia and the dictionary.

SA — Sturmabteilung or storm troopers or Paramilitary organization. They were known as the Brown Shirted Storm Troopers.

Scheveningen — Beach on the outskirts of The Hague

Tante — Dutch for Aunt

The Netherlands — Also commonly called 'Holland' because of the Provinces with the most population is in North and South Holland Province.

Vader — Dutch for Father

VE Day — Victory in Europe Day (V-E Day or VE Day) commemorates May 8, 1945. It is the date when the World War II Allies formally accepted the unconditional surrender of the armed forces of Nazi Germany and the end of Adolf Hitler's Third Reich.

visa — Foreign citizens wishing to immigrate and live permanently in a country must obtain a visa by complying with immigration laws.

Wehrmacht — It was the unified armed forces of Germany from 1935 to 1945. It consisted of the army, navy and air force.

Yad Vashem — *Yad Vashem* is a memorial authority in Jerusalem established by the Holocaust Martyrs' and Heroes' Remembrance Law adopted by the Israeli Knesset (Parliament) on August 19, 1953.

References

Reference code used in the figures, photographs, and charts are in brackets { }.

BOOKS

Bartlett, John — *Familiar Quotation* (http://www.amazon.com/Bartletts-Familiar-Quotations-Fifteenth-Anniversary/dp/B0020AVI54), Fifteenth and 125 Anniversary Edition, Little, Brown and Company, Boston, 1980.

Berenbaum, Michael — *The World Must Know - The History of the Holocaust as told in the United States Holocaust Memorial Museum* (http://www.amazon.com/The-World-Must-Know-Holocaust/dp/080188358X), Second Edition – Johns Hopkins University Press, 1933.

Gilbert, Martin — *Never Again-A History of the Holocaust* (http://www.amazon.com/Never-Again-The-History-Holocaust/dp/0789304090), Universe Publishing, NY, before 2005, {NA}.

Krell, Robert — *Children Holocaust Survivors Memories and Reflections* (http://www.amazon.com/Child-Holocaust-Survivors-Memories-Reflections/dp/1425137202), Trafford Publishing, Victoria, BC, Canada, 2007, which can be purchased on Amazon.com. {RK}

Oliner, Samuel P. and Pearl M. — *The Altruistic Personality-Rescuers of Jews in Nazi Europe* (http://www.amazon.com/Altruistic-Personality-Rescuers-Jews-Europe/dp/0029238293), The Free Press, a division of Macmillan, Inc, NY, 1992.[117]

Warmbrunn, Werner — *The Dutch under German Occupation 1940-1945* (http://www.amazon.com/Dutch-Under-German-Occupation-1940-1945/dp/0804701520), Stanford University Press, Stanford, California, 1963.[118]

The American Heritage Dictionary — *Second College Edition* (http://www.amazon.com/The-American-Heritage-Dictionary-College/dp/0395329442), Houghton Mifflin Company, Boston, 1982.

---

[117] This book is compiled from my parents interview and 700 others, at Humboldt State University. The results were published in their book.

[118] Most of the source of the information in this book is from The Netherlands State Institute of War Documentation in Amsterdam, which since 1945, has been collecting on behalf of the Dutch government great quantities of data and documents dealing with the history of The Netherlands during the Second World War.

INTERNET SOURCES

The Holocaust and History: Introduction to the Survivors Stories, by Lawrence N. Powell, Tulane University — http://www.holocaustsurvivors.org/data.show.php?di=record&da=texts&ke=6.

Ancestry (http://home.ancestry.com/)— I organized and input the family information as I received photos and information from family. I reference this for family confirmations of names and dates. Obtained copies of ship embarkation documents.

Wikipedia (http://www.wikipedia.org/)— is a free encyclopedia on the internet. Since this source is a compiled contribution of various authors the facts may not been verified. The main subjects I researched were Final Solution, WWI, WWII, Germany, Hitler, Israel, and Treaty of Versailles. {Wiki}.

PHOTOGRAPHS SOURCES

Robert Krell {K}

Blank/No Code Oversloot Family — Jeannette, Johanna, Jack, Jenny or Julia.

Courtesy of — The name of the family member in England and The Netherlands that provided the photo.

U.S. Holocaust Memorial Museum (http://www.ushmm.org/) — United States Holocaust Memorial Museum each photography will indicate donor by "courtesy of xx" in the caption. The USHMM licensed image reproduction used are "The views of opinions expressed in this (book/Articles/Exhibit/other), and the context in which the images are used, do not necessarily reflect the views or policy of, nor imply approval, or endorsement by, the United States Holocaust Memorial Museum."

JACOB OVERSLOOT SOURCES

In an attempt to give the reader the most accurate information about World War II in my dad's own words, I mix paragraphs and sentences of the three sources below. Words in italics in the book are from one or combination of these sources.

Speech in 1976 — Jacob Oversloot written speech for the Pasadena Jewish Temple and Center congregation on January 9, 1977 at 10am, organized by Hy Vego, Chairman of the Adult Education Committee. It is the only English written history I found in my dad's words.

Note: The two interviews below were difficult to translate because Dad was hard of hearing and he spoke half Dutch and half English. Also Dutch grammar was used and the placement of the subject and verb was sometimes reversed. Some words may not be exact but the spirit of the thoughts are accurate.

Audio Only Interview 1984 (http://collections.ushmm.org/search/catalog/irn510798) — Dad was invited to a "Faith In Humankind: Rescuers of the Jews During the Holocaust" conference held in Washington DC on September 17-19, 1984. As part of the conference, they recorded an oral history of each of the participants. The original CD is located in the United States Holocaust Memorial Museum ("USHMM") archives. Reference number is RG 50.157.022.

Video Interview 1987 — Gay Block and Malka Drucker interviewed Dad and Martha (Dad's second wife) on June 5, 1987 at their home at 3500 Glenrose, Altadena, Ca. Their interview was provided to the Yad Vashem Holocaust Memorial Museum in Israel. I received the DVD through my contact with Michlean Amir, Reference Archivist, at the museum on April 17, 2009. Reference is RG-50.012*0068.[119]

---

119 This interview and 700 others were used for the Altruistic Personality project directed by Samuel and Pearl Oliner, at Humboldt State University. The results were published in their book, The Altruistic Personality – Rescuers of Jews in Nazi Europe, which I referenced from time to time.

Index